Written by Sally A Jones and Amanda C Jones
Front Cover Photo by Annalisa Jones

Published by GUINEA PIG EDUCATION

2 Cobs Way,
New Haw,
Addlestone,
Surrey,
KT15 3AF.
www.guineapigeducation.co.uk

ISBN: 978-0-9558315-5-3

Dear Kids,

Now you have worked your way through Creative Story Writing, Persuasive Writing and Argument and Information Writing in the 'Teach Your Child Good English' series, you are ready to brush up on your grammar and punctuation skills.

Work through the exercises again and again, until you are familiar with them. It will be worth it. Put a smile on your teacher's face. Do not forget to use good spelling, punctuation and grammar in your written work.

To Parents,

As your child develops his or her written work, spelling and punctuation mistakes will start to matter more. Marks will be lost in examinations. Get your child into good habits now. This book focuses on specific concepts that children find especially hard to grasp. The writer, an experienced teacher and tutor for over 20 years, is aware that many children make the same mistakes. They confuse homophones: their, there and they're, for example. By making your child aware of these tricky areas, they will be able to correct their own work.

PART ONE

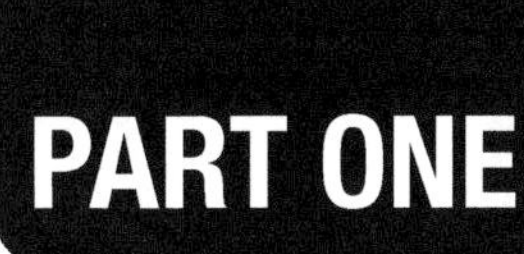

Challenge One

Let us brush up on when we use

CAPITAL LETTERS

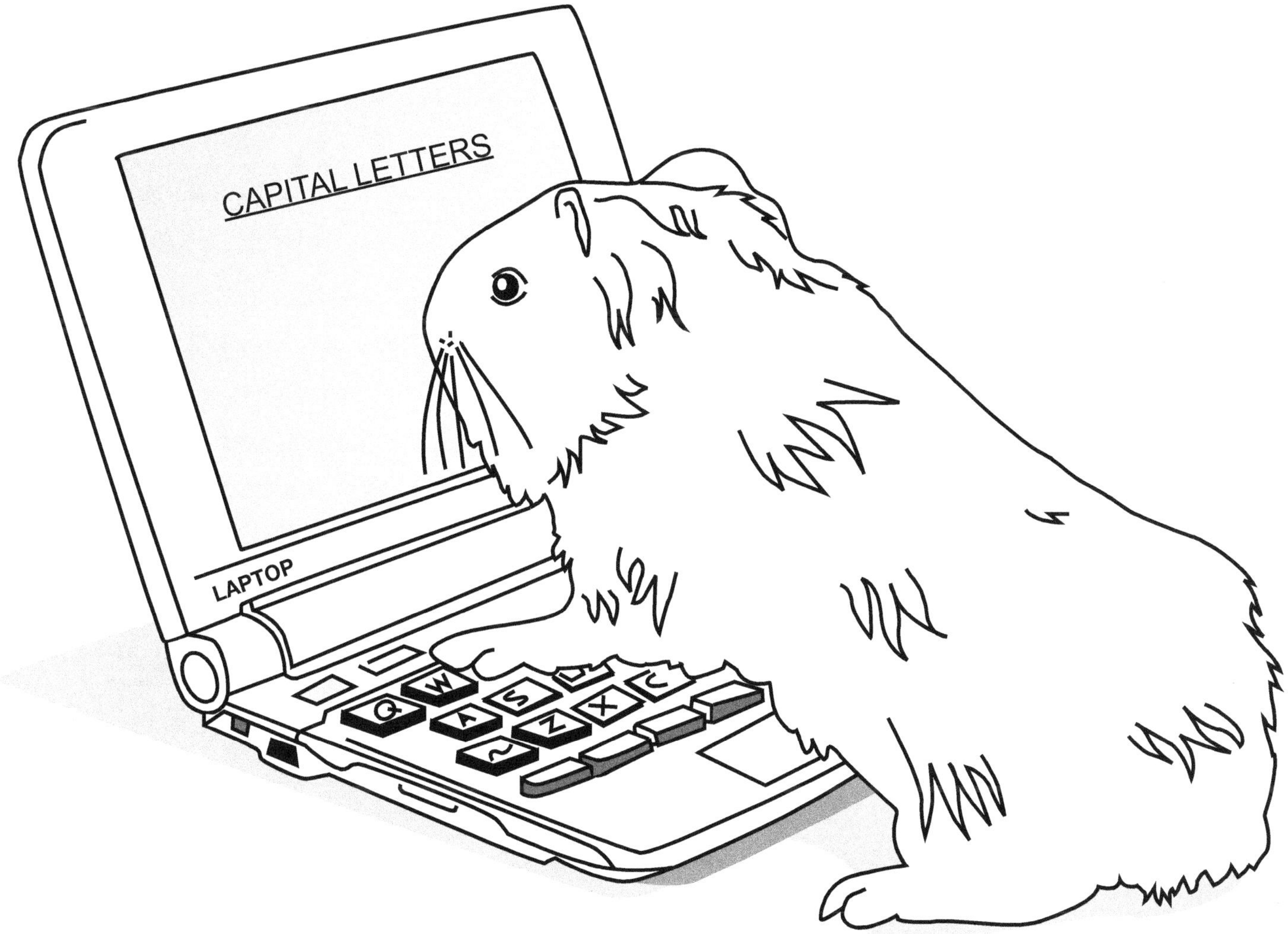

Check up on capitals.

Proper nouns have capital letters:

***M**rs Jones*	***S**am*	***L**ucy*	***G**ran*
***D**ad*	***J**et*	***F**luff*	***M. A. S**mith*
***M**rs **R**obinson*	***G**eneral **J**ameson*	***D**octor **S.A. S**aunders*	

Find some more names and titles.

Sentences begin with capital letters:

- ***A**my likes to play with her toys.*
- ***P**aul has a large collection of computer games.*

Write some more sentences. Take care to put in the capital letters.

Capital letters are needed in letters.

32 **F**airview Road,
Rushford,
Middlesex.
2nd **J**anuary

Dear **L**aura,

Thank you for my lovely birthday present. It was very kind of you.

Love from,

Gabriella

Write a letter, taking care to put in the capital letters.

Abbreviations are letters that stand for longer names.

B.B.C British Broadcasting Corporation

R.S.V.P ....

C.O.D ....

M.B.E ....

Find some more abbreviations and their meanings.

Days of the week, months of the year, names of holidays and religious days need capital letters.

Write in some more names that belong to this set.

***M**onday*	***T**uesday*	***J**anuary*	***F**ebruary*
***D**ecember 12th*	***C**hristmas **D**ay*	***E**aster*	***S**t. **P**atrick's **D**ay*

Titles of books, music and magazines need capital letters.

***A**lice in **W**onderland by **L**ewis **C**arroll*

***T**he **T**imes* ***T**he **D**aily **M**ail*

***T**he **A**dventures of **P**addington **B**ear by **M**ichael **B**ond*

List some more books or newspapers. Take care to put in the capital letters.

Names of villages, towns, cities, counties, countries and continents all need capital letters.

***L**aleham*	***A**shford*	***S**taines*	***L**ondon*
***M**iddlesex*	***C**olwyn **B**ay*	***B**ournemouth*	***A**frica*
***A**ustralia*	*an **A**frican chief*	*a **F**rench girl*	*an **E**skimo child*

Names of rivers, oceans, canals and mountains all have capital letters.

***T**he **G**rand **U**nion **C**anal*	***M**ount **E**verest*	***M**ount **S**nowdon*
***R**iver **T**hames*	***R**iver **N**ile*	***A**tlantic **O**cean*
***I**ndian **O**cean*	***T**he **L**ake **D**istrict*	***T**he **A**lps*
***T**he **P**yrenees*	....	....

List some more on this page.

Names of streets need capital letters.

***F**airview **R**oad*	***T**he **R**oyal **M**ews*	***C**hurch **R**oad*
***H**igh **S**treet*	***A**cacia **D**rive*	***O**xford **S**treet*

List some more on this page.

Names of schools, parks, buildings and castles need capital letters.

***C**astle **H**ill **F**irst **S**chool*	***H**arrods*	***H**yde **P**ark*
***T**he **S**even **B**ridge*	***W**indsor **C**astle*	***T**esco*
***B**uckingham **P**alace*	***T**he **L**ammas **P**ark*	***M**c **D**onald's*
***T**he **R**ose and **C**rown*	***A**shford **H**ospital*	***T**he **P**ortland **B**ill*
***D**artford **T**unnel*	***G**reat **O**rmond **S**treet **H**ospital*	

List some more on this page.

Names of political parties and religious bodies need capital letters.

***T**he **L**abour **P**arty*	***C**onservatives*	***T**he **P**ope*
***G**od*	***C**hristianity*	***J**esus **C**hrist*
***A**llah*	***B**uddhism*	***T**he **D**alai **L**ama*
***H**induism*	***I**slam*	***J**udaism*

The deities of all religions have capital letters.

The Holy Bible, Qur'an and other holy books also all have capital letters.

Names of organisations need capital letters...

***T**he **F**oreign **L**egion*	***T**he **C**ivil **S**ervice*	***T**he **B**rownies*
***T**he **R**oyal **A**ir **F**orce*	***T**he **S**couts*	***T**he **G**irl **G**uides*

and specific brands...

***B**.**M**.**X** bikes*	***K**ellogg's*	***M**ars*
***V**auxhall*	***W**alker's crisps*	***C**adbury*

and planets in the solar system.

***M**ars*	***V**enus*	***J**upiter*

Names of historical periods or events need capital letters.

***T**he **T**udors*	***T**he **B**attle of **H**astings*
***T**he **G**eorgian **P**eriod*	***T**he **S**econd **W**orld **W**ar*

The pronoun ‘I’ used alone needs a capital letter.

*Charlotte and **I** both had a drink but **I** had a cream cake as well.*

Write some more sentences using I...

At the beginning of a quotation we use a capital letter.

*Mum said, “**P**lease wash your hands for dinner.”*

Write some more sentences with speech. Take care to put in capital letters.

Write out these sentences putting in capital letters.

1. I go to castle hill school.
2. My best friend is paul.
3. there are three boys called Matthew in my class.
4. I live in fairbridge road in kingston.
5. For my birthday treat I went to lego land in windsor.
6. I like reading harry potter by j.k. rowling.
7. In my road there is a church called kingsbury methodist church.
8. Chloe and i went for a walk.
9. I go shopping on friday with my mum.
10. In march it will be easter.
11. Our new rabbit is called benjy.

Challenge Two

Let us brush up on how to

WRITE SENTENCES

<u>Capital</u> Letters

Capital letters are used:

- to begin a sentence
- to write a person's name
- for the name of a pet
- for initials
- for addresses
- for the name of places
- for the name of organisations
- for days of the week
- for months and holidays
- for titles of books and newspapers
- to begin lines of a poem

Write an example for each one.

Correct this sentence:

When James went to London, he visited buckingham palace and the houses of parliament.

Did you know that:

- A name is a proper noun - *Mrs Jones*
- Common nouns - *dog, pencil*
- Abstract nouns - *love, peace, joy*
- Collective nouns - *a bunch of flowers*

Sentences are made <u>*VERY EASY*</u>...

What is a sentence?

You will probably answer:

It is a group of words which start with a capital letter and end with a full stop.

<u>This is correct</u> 

Did you know that there are four different types of sentence?

STATEMENTS	QUESTIONS
Spiders make webs.	*What is that on the wall?*

COMMANDS	EXCLAMATIONS
Catch that spider. *Meet me at six.*	*Help me!*

Write your own examples for each one.

Each sentence has a subject and some action (a predicate).

__I__ am scared of spiders.

__Tom__ is frightened of snakes.

Tom and I are both subjects.

The action parts of these sentences use the verbs scared or frightened, to show how they feel.

One more important thing you need to know, is the way sentences are made up.

1. If I say,

Tom saw a spider.

I have written a MAIN CLAUSE (it can be a sentence by itself).

2. Now, I can add more SUBORDINATE CLAUSES or 'SUB-CLAUSES' to make the original sentence more interesting:

Tom saw an enormous spider, which was crawling across the bath.

The subordinate clause cannot be a sentence by itself.

3. I can add a clause to the main clause at the end of my sentence, at the beginning or in the middle.

Seeing an enormous spider, Tom leapt out of the bath.

Tom, who was terrified of spiders, saw a spider in the bath.

4. Connectives like 'which' and 'who' have been used to join the clauses together.

1. Write a sentence about Sophie and a snake with one clause.

2. Write 3 more sentences adding 'sub-clauses' to the beginning, middle and end of the sentences.

Finally...

You do not have to be boring and write only **simple sentences**.

- *I hate big spiders.*
- *I like slimy frogs.*

Make your work interesting by using **compound sentences**, joining your ideas together with connectives like ‘and’ or ‘but’.

- *I hate big spiders, but I pick up slimy frogs.*

Or, even more interesting by using **complex sentences**.

- *Seeing the enormous spider, Sophie screamed hysterically.*
- *Crawling through the tall grass, I saw a long grass snake.*

Write this passage out in your exercise book. Make these simple sentences more interesting. Turn them into compound or complex sentences, by adding connectives or subordinate clauses.

Sophie was in the garden. She saw a snake. It was in the grass. It slithered. She was scared. She called out for her Mum. They rang the wildlife rescue service. A man caught the snake. He said that it was only a harmless grass snake. He took it away.

....

....

....

....

....

....

....

....

Now check your sentences with this suggested answer.

Sophie, who was helping in the garden, saw a green snake slithering through the long grass. Feeling scared, she called out for her mum and they rang the wildlife rescue service. Catching the snake, the man said that it was only a harmless grass snake but he took it away.

"There are two ways of writing a sentence."

For example:

1. A creepy house stood on the top of the hill.
2. On the top of the hill, stood a creepy house.

Complete the following sentences:

1. The two girls went to the theatre last weekend.

   Last ....

2. Without looking to see if there were any cars coming, Emily raced across the road.

   Emily ....

3. The fair was cancelled due to the heavy rain.

   Due ....

4. The brightly coloured boats bobbed up and down on the sea.

   ....

Here are some examples of connectives or joining words (conjunctions):

They will help you write longer sentences.

if	but	so	whilst
because	while	before	yet
or	as	and	unless
when	since	till	after
until	whenever	besides	

Here are some more interesting connectives:

however	therefore	meanwhile	nevertheless
whereas	so that	even though	furthermore
on the other hand	although	in order that	neither
because of	due to	as a result of	provided that
in my opinion	according to	in spite of this	in addition to

Connectives join clauses or sentences together to make more *complex sentences*...

Underline the connectives in these sentences:

The dog was hungry **so** it growled viciously.

1. You can have a pet dog if you promise to walk it every day.
2. The athletes started running before the whistle had been blown.
3. I hummed a song while I waited for the bus.
4. I am the oldest therefore I should sit in the front of the car.
5. Our car is clean whereas his car is still dirty.
6. The test was difficult although I had revised.
7. The outing was enjoyable because the sun was shining.
8. The tennis match was delayed until the rain stopped.

Write the following sentences out, putting in the most suitable connective.

until	*if*	*although*	*before*	*since*	*as*
so that	*when*	*where*	*so*	*whenever*	*while*

1. The show had an interval .... we could buy some refreshments.
2. The children were excited .... it snowed.
3. I took my umbrella to the shops .... it started to rain.
4. Sophie went on holiday to Spain .... she did not like flying.
5. I could get some popcorn .... the film starts.
6. We were arguing .... Mum told us to stop.
7. I will help you with your homework .... you tidy my room.
8. Rahan became very scared .... he passed the creepy house.

Now, choose a suitable ending for these sentences:

I visited the London Eye...	so I do not go to theme parks.
I emailed my friend...	before I visited her.
Sam was happy...	when I dressed up as a clown.
Dad shouted at me...	as he was going on holiday.
I have refused to eat apples...	after I had been to the Tower of London.
My friends giggled...	because I broke the window.
I do not like fast rides...	since I found a maggot in one.

“**A connective can be a single word or more than one.**”

For example:

1. I will feed the cat so that he does not get hungry.

Choose the correct ending for each sentence:

The crowd left the stadium...	in order to see over the fence.
I finished my homework on Friday...	if you want to get good results.
I stood on a chair...	until I felt sick.
Work hard...	after the match had finished.
I ate jelly and ice cream...	so she bought both pairs of jeans.
Sophie could not decide...	so that I could go out on the weekend.

Join the main clause to the suitable sub-clause.

MAIN CLAUSE	SUB-CLAUSE
The boy won a medal,	as it leaned over the gate.
The girl apologised	because she was late.
The cat purred softly	to her friend's party.
The class listened attentively	that was flying to Chicago.
I stroked Becky's horse	when it saw its owner.
I can pick you up from the airport	for rescuing his friend.
We observed the rescue helicopter	hovering over the sea.
The old man was badly injured	so he was taken to hospital.
The robber was arrested	for stealing jewellery.
The plane left on time	to protect her baby from the hot sun.
Lucy shivered	if you tell me what time you will arrive.
The celebrity looked glamorous	as she stood in the rain.
The mother put up a sun shade	wearing a red dress.
Sacha received an invitation	as the ship was in trouble.
The sailors sent up a flare	while the headmaster spoke.

Challenge Three

Let us brush up on

PUNCTUATION

<u>Speech Marks</u> show the words someone is saying.

This is wrong.

Before leaving anita said thank you for a lovely holiday aunt muriel. ✗

This is correct.

Before leaving Anita said,
"Thank you for a lovely holiday, Aunt Muriel." ✔

Please can you pass me the sugar Charlotte requested her mother. 

"Please can you pass me the sugar, Charlotte?" requested her mother. 

"Question marks or full stops always come before the final speech mark."

"Each new speaker starts a new line."

Put speech marks in these sentences.

1. Would you like to come to my house for dinner? said Darren.
2. Sophie slammed the door and shouted it is not fair, everyone else will be at the party. Her mum replied you have not finished your homework.

Question Marks come at the end of a question.

How old are you?

Do you want to come to my house on Thursday?

Have you finished your homework?

Which of the following sentences are questions and which are statements?

1.	Is that your dog over there	☐
2.	Your cat has caught a mouse	☐
3.	Do you have any brothers or sisters	☐
4.	What do you want to do when you leave school	☐
5.	A policeman would be an exciting job	☐
6.	Are you going abroad when you go on holiday	☐

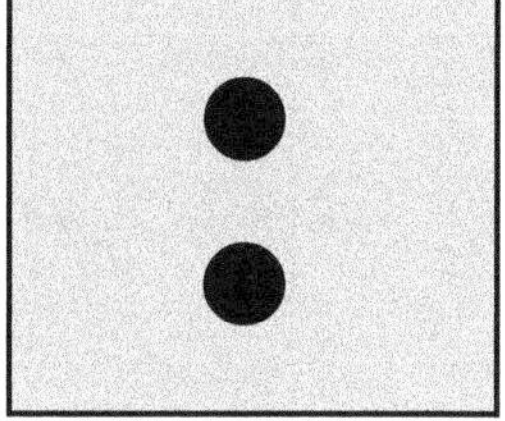

Colon - there are different ways you can use a colon.

1. to introduce a list of items or a quotation.

   There are many African animals in the zoo: elephants, giraffes, zebras, lions and gazelles.

2. to explain what has been said in the first clause of a sentence.

   I saw an elephant in the zoo that had small ears and smooth skin: it had come from India.

   The second part of this sentence explains why the elephant had small ears and smooth skin - it was a species of elephant from India.

Semi-Colon - there are also different ways you can use a semi-colon.

1. to separate long lists of items.

   I bought quite a few things from the airport shop: a book to read on the plane; a travel adaptor so I could charge my phone when I arrived in Greece; and suntan lotion which I had forgotten to pack.

2. to separate two ideas not joined by a conjunction (joining word)

   We visited the airport shop; we usually buy presents there.

   We went to the superstore; it always has good bargains.

   In both examples, the second statement is strongly linked to the meaning of the first one and adds further information.

Exclamation Mark

An exclamation is a statement said loudly, perhaps in anger.

Help! *Be quiet!* *Open the window!*

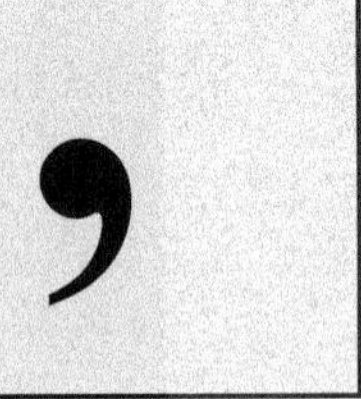

Commas - there are different ways you can use a comma.

1. to separate items in a list.

   At the restaurant I purchased pizza, salad and garlic bread.

2. to make a pause in a long sentence.

   There was such a big selection of pizzas on the menu, that I chose the dish of the day recommended by the chef.

3. to separate clauses.

   The restaurant, which is in the centre of town, is very popular in the summer.

4. after an adverb in a sentence.

   Thankfully, the pizza restaurant stayed open late.

Singular Apostrophe is used to show belonging and goes before the s.

Lucy's doll.

The doll belongs to Lucy.

The boy's car.

The car belongs to the boy.

Put the apostrophe into these sentences.

1. **Mum's** shopping bag was very heavy.
2. The girls teddy was very soft.
3. Grandads dog barked loudly.
4. Kims jumper was itchy.
5. Sams kite soared high in the sky.
6. Dads car went very fast.

Plural Apostrophe is used when an item belongs to more than one person and goes after the s...

The dogs' kennel.

The ladies' coats.

... but if the plural word does not end in an s, the apostrophe is used like this.

The children's toys

The men's cars

The firemen's hoses

Put in the missing apostrophes.

Singular

1. The **girl's** dress
2. The boys pen
3. A days work
4. The mans car
5. The womans glove
6. The childs clothes

Plural

1. The **girls'** dresses
2. The ladies bags
3. The boys pencils
4. Seven days work

But... when the plural does not end in 's'

1. The **men's** pipes
2. The womens gloves
3. The childrens clothes

The apostrophe is used as a <u>*contraction*</u>.

Can't is short for cannot.

Doesn't is short for does not.

The apostrophe is placed where the letter is missed out.

Write these abbreviated words in full:

can't	couldn't	don't	didn't	hasn't
he'd	haven't	he'll	he's	I'll
I'd	I'm	isn't	it's	I've
o'clock	shan't	she'll	o'er	that's
shouldn't	we'll	there's	they'll	we've
whate'er	where'er	whosoe'er	who've	wouldn't
you'll	you're			

Put in the apostrophe:

neednt	....	youll	....
Ive	....	o clock	....
dont	....	tis	....

Write the following sentence making use of the apostrophe as an abbreviation:

We will probably arrive at seven of the clock.

Challenge Four

Let us brush up on

PARTS OF SPEECH

Underline the verbs and adverbs in these sentences.

The baby **chuckled** (verb) **happily** (adverb).

1. The dog snored loudly on the rug.
2. In the test, the students scribbled hurriedly.
3. The eagle swooped aggressively at its prey.
4. The politician argued skilfully.
5. The audience waited expectantly for the film to start.
6. Richard read his book eagerly.
7. The athlete raced energetically past the finish line.
8. Dad shouted angrily at Kim.
9. A fox crept cunningly into the garden.
10. The boat swayed violently on the waves.

Find a noun, adjective, verb and adverb in these sentences. Write them in the chart below.

1. The ferocious dog barked loudly at the people who opened the gate.
2. The little brown mouse crept softly through the grass.
3. The huge stripy tiger prowled proudly through the jungle.
4. The cute rabbit ran playfully round the room.
5. The ginger cat watched the mouse hole attentively everyday.

ADJECTIVE	NOUN	VERB	ADVERB
ferocious	dog	barked	loudly
....	....	....	....
....	....	....	....
....	....	....	....
....	....	....	....

Write some more simply, super sentences with nouns, verbs, adjectives and adverbs.

Underline the verb or action word - for example, *'ran'*

1. The sneaky cat crept out of the open door.
2. The greedy cat gobbled up the chicken.
3. The lazy dog dozed in the sun all day.
4. The fat dog squeezed through the hole and got stuck.
5. The slimy frog croaked in the lily pond.

Now use adverbs with your verbs to make super sentences.

Underline the adverb that describes the verb.

1. The curious cat crept stealthily out of the open door.
2. The greedy cat quickly gobbled up the cooked chicken.
3. The lazy dog dozed peacefully in the sun.
4. The fat dog squeezed awkwardly through the hole.
5. The slimy frog croaked loudly in the lily pond.

Now make up sentences of your own.

Can you put the adjectives and nouns together?

ADJECTIVE	NOUN	
interesting	garden	interesting book
agreeable	walk	....
beautiful	book	....
fast	morning	....
delicious	dress	....
enjoyable	house	....
fine	car	....
mischievous	burger	....
pretty	toddler	....
pleasant	film	....

Remember, it is important to make your sentences more interesting by using adjectives with your nouns.

ADD A NOUN	ADD AN ADJECTIVE	
a cat	a sneaky cat	a greedy cat
a dog	a lazy dog	a fat dog
a frog	a jumpy frog	slimy frog

Word Practice

Write the examples. Use nouns and adjectives to make phrases.

Give each animal or noun two describing words or adjectives.

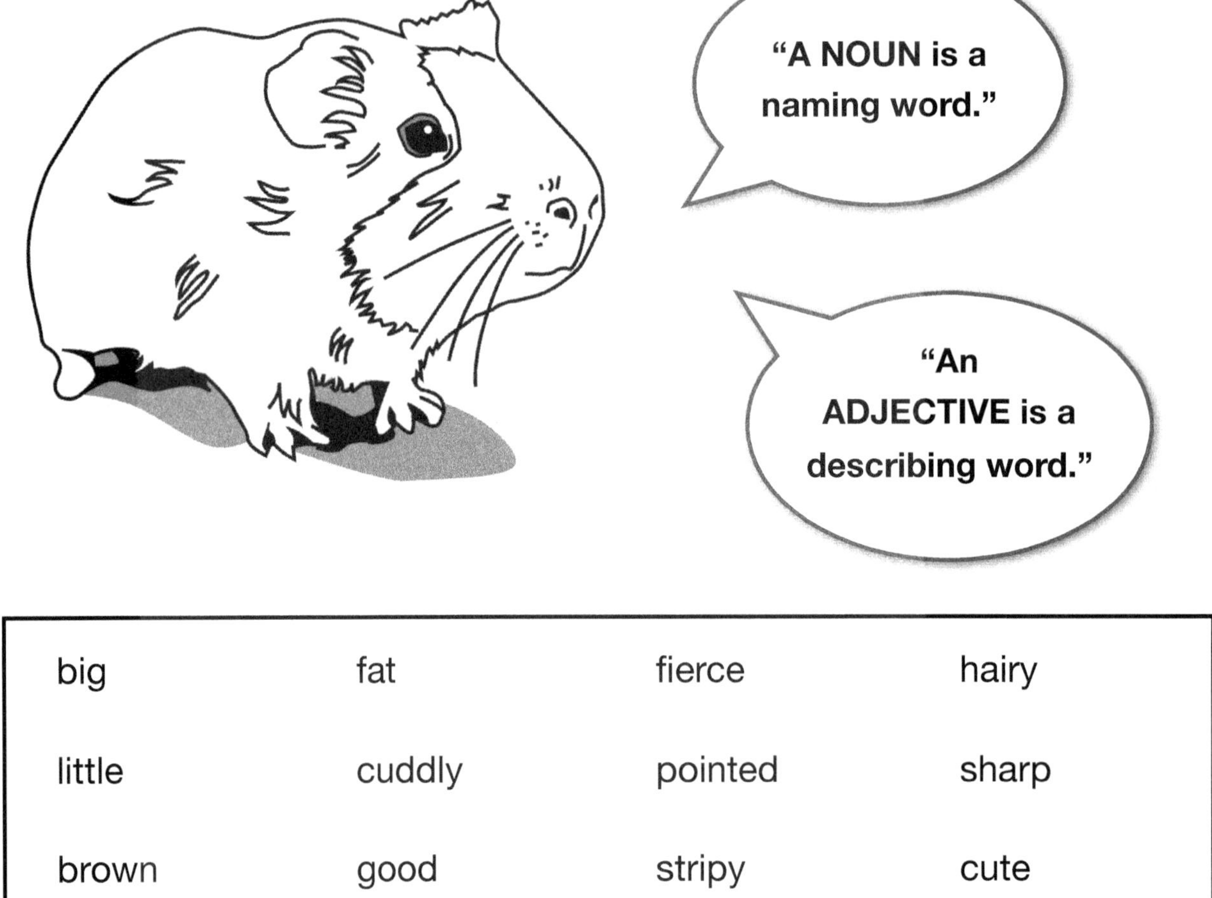

big	fat	fierce	hairy
little	cuddly	pointed	sharp
brown	good	stripy	cute
Easter	furry		

MOUSE	....	....
CAT	....	....
DOG	....	....
RABBIT	....	....
TIGER	....	....

Can you think of any more adjectives to describe these nouns?

Match the verb with the most suitable adverb.

There is more than one choice.

VERB	ADVERB
walk	ravenously
argue	happily
arrive	bravely
stroll	energetically
eat	politely
growl	respectfully
watch	aimlessly
knock	ferociously
wait	loudly
act	recklessly
sneak	badly
follow	deeply
care	closely
love	patiently
shout	furtively
volunteer	flatly
fight	faithfully
behave	tirelessly
answer	tenderly
interrupt	suspiciously
live	quickly
jump	aggressively
refuse	promptly
treat	dangerously
gobble	rudely
drive	loudly
work	greedily

Use the words in the box to fill in the blanks.

pleaded	exclaimed	muttered
whispered	responded	shouted
screamed	explained	uttered

1. The man .... that he would help me.
2. The boy .... why he was late.
3. The girl .... quietly to her friend.
4. The toddler .... loudly.
5. The girl .... that she was sorry.
6. I .... with Dad to let me go to the sleepover.

"Use these verbs instead of 'said' to make your writing more interesting."

Can you think of any more?

Test Yourself

Turn these nouns into describing words or adjectives.

1. A road with many stones is a ....stony.... road.
2. A man of great wealth is a .... man.
3. A meal with a nice taste is a .... meal.

An **<u>ACTIVE VERB</u>** is underlined in the sentence below.

The girl <u>ate</u> the chocolate bar.

The subject of this sentence is 'the girl' so she does the action.

A **<u>PASSIVE VERB</u>** is underlined in the sentence below.

The chocolate bar <u>was eaten</u> by the girl.

In this sentence, the chocolate bar is the subject and has the action done to it.

Write the following sentences using passive verbs.

Sam broke the vase.
The vase was broken by Sam.

1. The decorator painted the wall.

   ....

2. The cat pounced on the mouse.

   The mouse was ....

3. The racing drivers drove the car.

   The car was ....

4. The robber burgled the house.

   The house was ....

5. The heavy rain caused a flood.

   The flood was ....

We do not need to repeat nouns or naming words because we can use pronouns. They take the place of peoples' names and become the subject.

FIRST PERSON	SECOND PERSON	THIRD PERSON
I	you	he/she
we	your	it
my		they

SINGULAR PRONOUNS - I, she, he, it

PLURAL PRONOUNS - we, they

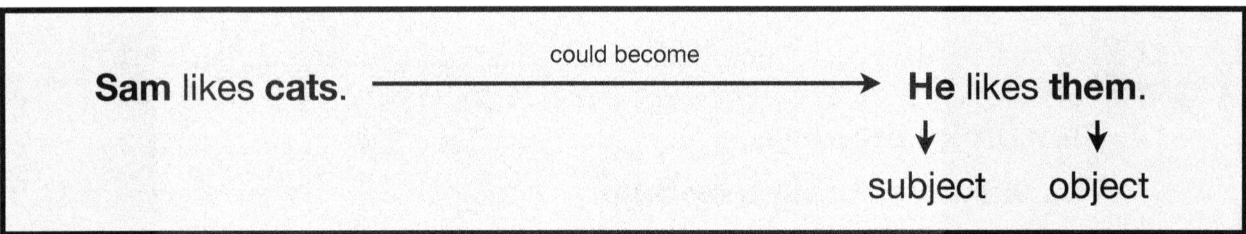

Some examples of pronouns...

PERSONAL: I, we, he, she, it, they, me, you

POSSESSIVE: ours, mine, yours, hers, his, its, theirs

RELATIVE: what, which, that, who, whom, whose

DEMONSTRATIVE: this, that, these, those

Replace the words in brackets with pronouns.

(Ben) .... walked into the classroom with (his mum) ....

They looked at (the pictures on the wall) ....,

"Which one is (your picture) ....?"

"That one is (my picture) ...."

The words below are prepositions. Prepositions come before a noun or pronoun and include:

above	about	across	against	in
round	from	into	below	along
after	behind	near	around	at
to	before	down	for	beneath
besides	beyond	by	of	on
over	since	except	towards	until
under	underneath	with	without	through

They often tell us something about time and place or the relationship between two words.

Look how they show the relationship between the verb and the noun. Choose a suitable pronoun from the box above to put in the spaces below.

1. The cat pounced ....on......... the fence.
2. We chased my dog .... the long grass.
3. Clare will be performing .... the show.
4. The people crossed the road .... the van.
5. He received a birthday card .... his best friend.

Finish the sentences, putting in the correct prepositions.

1. I am **ashamed of** the way my brother behaved in class.
2. I took the **blame for** the broken vase.
3. I will not **comment on** my appalling exam results.
4. Compared .... my friend, I excelled at history.
5. I was conscious .... a ghostly presence in the room.
6. I disagree .... the changes made by the new headteacher.
7. I was disappointed .... my teams performance.
8. I am disgusted .... people who drop litter in the street.
9. He was guilty .... a terrible crime.
10. I live opposite .... Mr. Smith.
11. He looks similar .... my dad.
12. She suffers .... a rare condition.
13. I will write .... my German friend.
14. I will eagerly wait .... some more news.

Revision on connectives

until *as if* *since* *in order to* *because*

1. .... I went to my new school, I have learnt how to play the flute.
2. I attended the ballet classes .... the end of term.
3. We know how the programme ended .... we watched it.
4. We worked fast .... finish the test.
5. He greeted me .... he had always known me.

Conjunctions can be used for:

TIME	PLACE	REASON FOR	OTHER
while	where	since	while
when	whenever	because	although
after			as
before			though
since			in order that
until			so that
whenever			except that
			as though

Can you think of any more?

Conjunctions can be used as connectives or joining words: joining clauses to their subordinate clauses.

Parts of speech include:

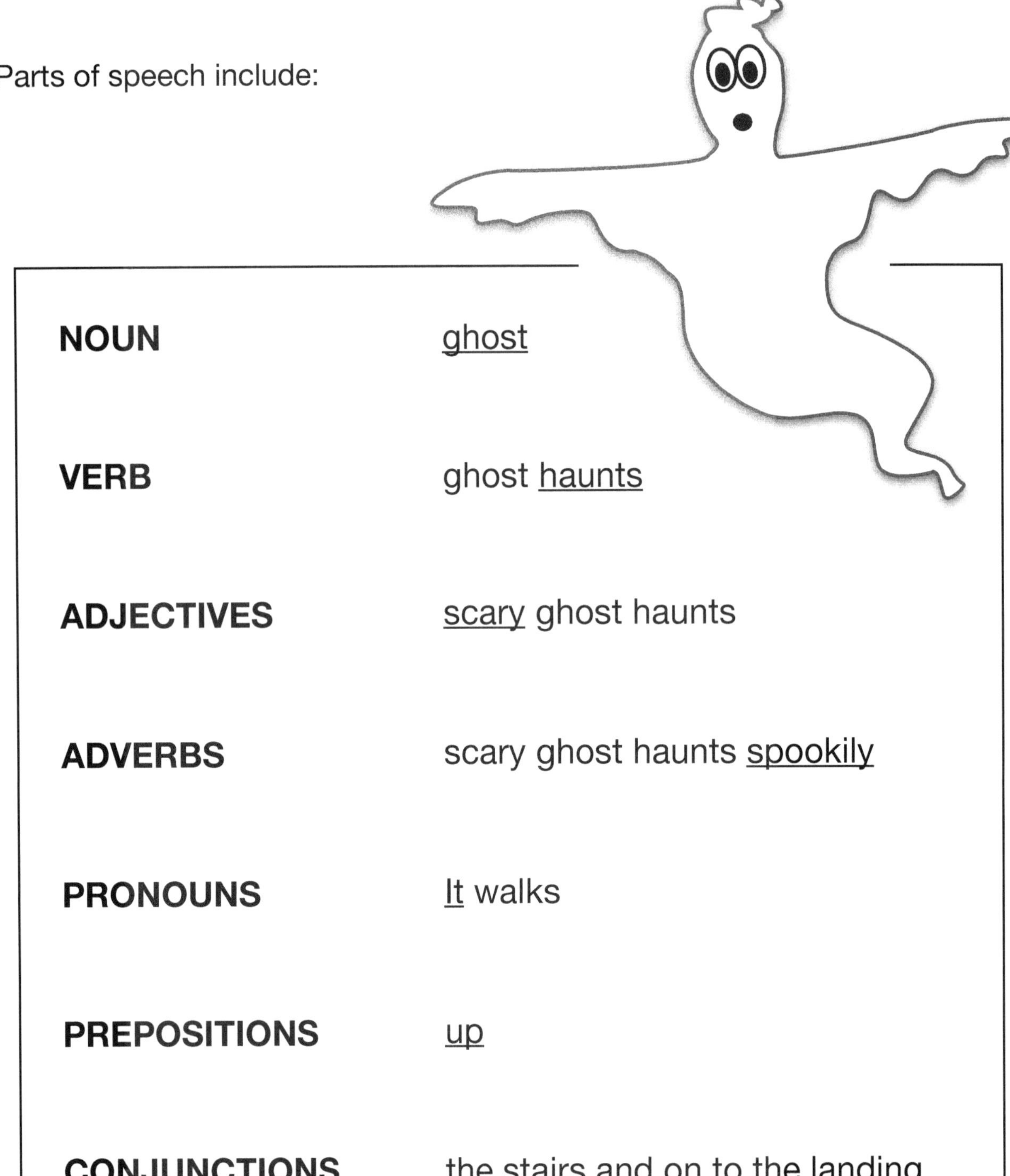

NOUN	ghost
VERB	ghost haunts
ADJECTIVES	scary ghost haunts
ADVERBS	scary ghost haunts spookily
PRONOUNS	It walks
PREPOSITIONS	up
CONJUNCTIONS	the stairs and on to the landing

The scary (*adjective*) ghost (*noun*) in (*preposition*) Hampton Court (*noun*) walks (*verb*) spookily (*adverb*) up (*preposition*) the stairs (*noun*) and (*conjunction*) across (*preposition*) the landing (*noun*).

‘Who’ and ‘which’ are <u>*relative pronouns*</u>.

- Use ‘who’ when writing about people.

  The girl, who fell over at school, was taken to hospital.

- Use ‘which’ when writing about things or animals.

  The stray kitten, which arrived at our door, did not have an owner.

“Spot the relative pronouns in the sentences below.”

1. The new book, which was on sale at midnight, sold hundreds of copies.
2. The boy found a necklace, which he took to the police.
3. The man, who rescued the drowning boy, received an award.
4. The cat, which was very hungry, greedily gobbled down his dinner.

Don't use *boring words* like ~~nice~~.

Instead use adjectives like:

fantastic beautiful agreeable fine

delicious convenient interesting amazing

Verbs like:

completed

concluded

are better than finish.

Verbs like:

received

obtained

are better than got.

Verbs like:

plodded

strolled

rambled

marched

hobbled

stamped

are better than walked.

Challenge Five

Let us brush up on our

LITERARY TECHNIQUES

Let's introduce some literary devices.

Similes *compare* using 'like' or 'as'

Match the similes

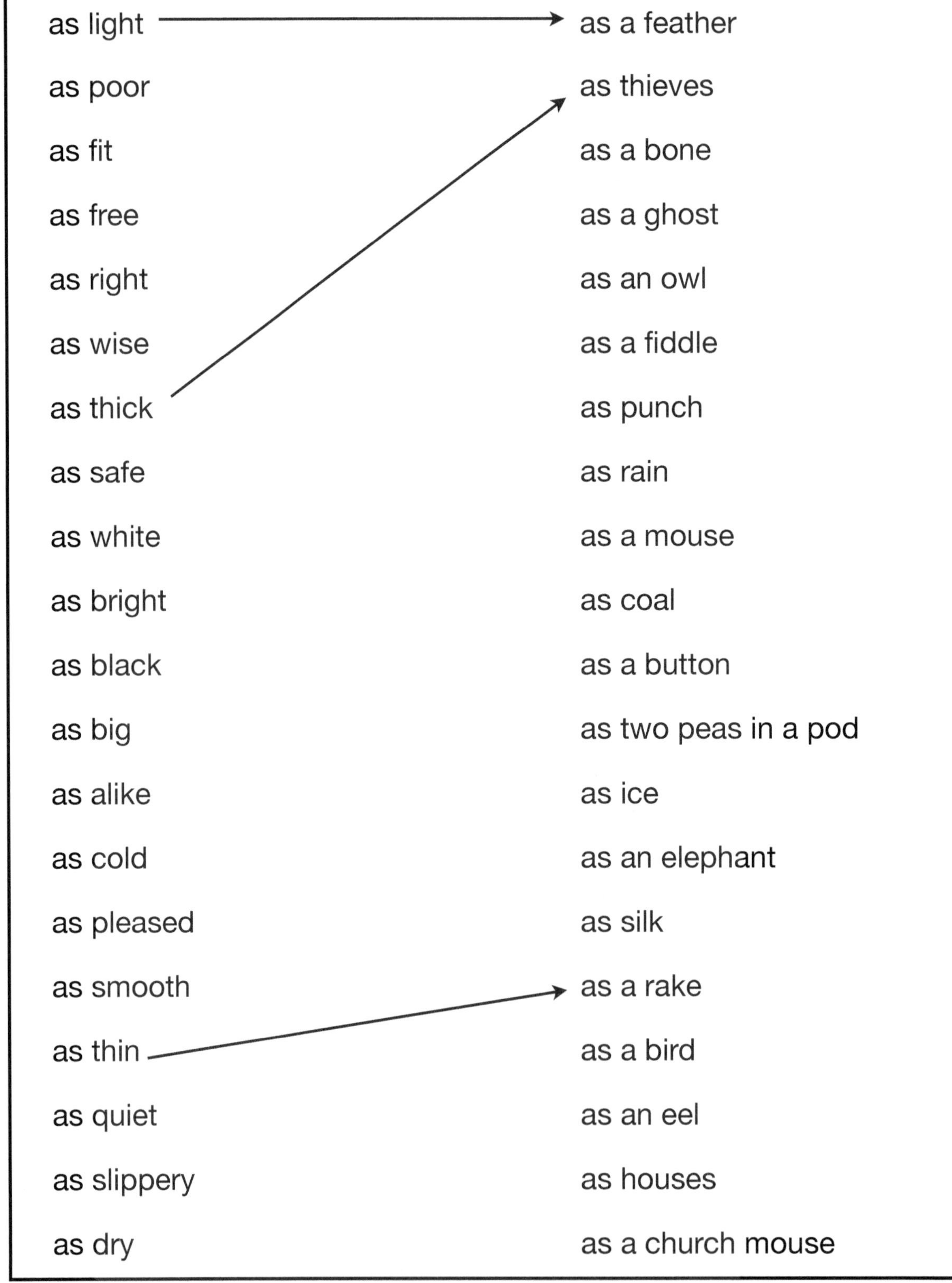

as light	as a feather
as poor	as thieves
as fit	as a bone
as free	as a ghost
as right	as an owl
as wise	as a fiddle
as thick	as punch
as safe	as rain
as white	as a mouse
as bright	as coal
as black	as a button
as big	as two peas in a pod
as alike	as ice
as cold	as an elephant
as pleased	as silk
as smooth	as a rake
as thin	as a bird
as quiet	as an eel
as slippery	as houses
as dry	as a church mouse

These similes are well known sayings but you can make up some of your own.

Metaphors _compare_ two things without using 'like' or 'as'.

Look at these examples:

- *The girl had a blond head of straw.*
- *The hair dryer is a growling dragon breathing out hot air.*
- *Jack's hungry guinea pig was the family lawn mower. His sharp teeth cut cleanly through every blade of grass.*

Alliteration is the _repetition of the initial sounds._

Look at these examples:

- *Sam smiled as he stood silently watching Sylvester, his pet guinea pig.*
- *The gorgeous guinea pig greedily gobbles the green grass.*

Personification gives _objects human qualities._

Look at this example:

- *The hungry sea devoured the beach.*

Onomatopoeia is when words _sound like the action being described._

Look at this example:

- *Snap, crunch, crackle went his sharp teeth on the grass.*

Challenge Six

Let us brush up on tricky spellings called

HOMOPHONES

"Do not let homophones confuse you."

What is a *homophone*?

Homophones are words that sound the same but have different spellings and meanings.

TO, TOO, TWO	HERE, HEAR
The greedy girl ate two hamburgers, when she went to the restaurant. She ate too much and felt very sick.	*Here is Tom. Can you hear him quarreling with his sister Sophie?*

WHERE, WERE	THREW, THROUGH
Where are Tom and Sophie? They were up to mischief as usual.	*The naughty boy threw the ball, right through the window into the house.*

THERE, THEIR, THEY'RE	*They're over there with their pet spider.*

To help you remember, underline two homophones in each sentence.

1. We go to the beach to see the sea.
2. When you make pizza, it is a great idea to grate the cheese.
3. A gentle breeze blew over the blue sea.
4. Some people think it feels right to write with their left hand.
5. The child knew where he had left his new toy.
6. We stand here so we can hear the music.
7. Whilst driving on his lunch break, the man had to brake sharply to avoid a dog.
8. The mail is delivered by male and female post workers.
9. Sit in peace and enjoy a piece of cake.
10. Mum buys a bunch of flowers and some flour to make a cake.
11. I will meet you by the cold meat counter at the supermarket.
12. I took my son for a holiday in the sun.
13. Have you read the gruesome tale about a dog which lost its tail?
14. We sew up the costumes quickly so we will be ready in time for the show.

Can you think of some more?

Remember:

A HOMONYM is a word that is spelt the same as another word but has a different meaning.

For example,

Bear - is an animal or it can mean carrying a weight.

I cannot bear to see a sad teddy bear.

The girl in the cream top ate strawberries and cream.

Now, write your own silly sentences to remember these homophones:

Homophones

Do you **know** them?

Yes or **no**...

SEE SEA	BEEN BEAN	FLOWER FLOUR
KNEW NEW	BLUE BLEW	RIGHT WRITE
TALE TAIL	GRATE GREAT	PIECE PEACE
MAIL MALE	HEAR HERE	SEW SO
BREAK BRAKE	MEAT MEET	SUN SON

Revision

Choose the correct homophone.

1. My new trousers are .... (blue, blew).
2. Beanos are my favourite .... (serial, cereal).
3. I cut a slice of .... (current, currant) cake.
4. I .... (hear, here) you are going on holiday.

PART TWO

"These pages will help to improve your English."

- Complete the exercises in neat handwriting.
- Write down the time this work took you to complete.

Exercise One

Vocabulary

Match the words with the correct meaning.

I and G - solitary means alone.

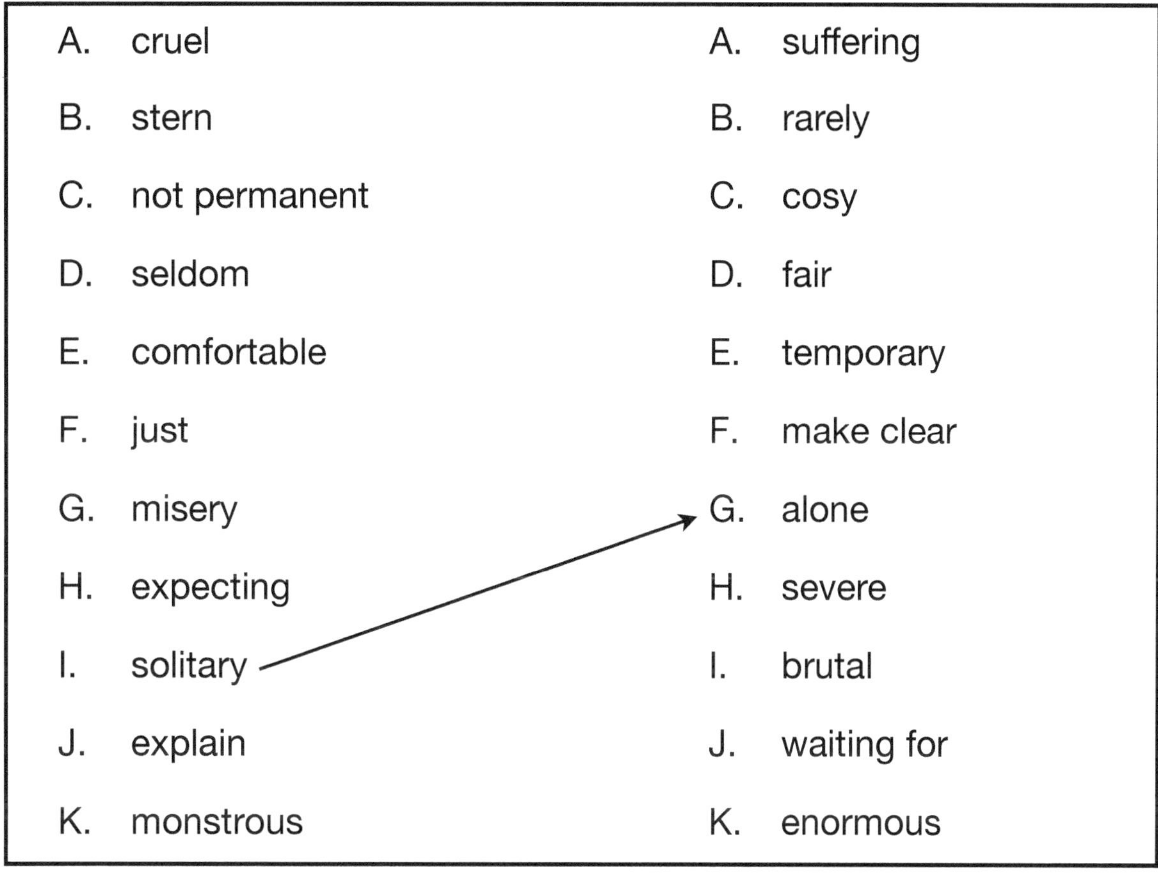

A.	cruel	A.	suffering
B.	stern	B.	rarely
C.	not permanent	C.	cosy
D.	seldom	D.	fair
E.	comfortable	E.	temporary
F.	just	F.	make clear
G.	misery	G.	alone
H.	expecting	H.	severe
I.	solitary	I.	brutal
J.	explain	J.	waiting for
K.	monstrous	K.	enormous

Copy out the sentences. Put in capital letters and full stops where they are needed.

1. Tim rides a brown horse its name is lady.
2. The ship was warned of the dangerous rocks by the portland bill lighthouse.
3. The book wind in the willows is written by Kenneth Graham.
4. Mum's birthday is on valentine's day which is the 14th February
5. Our new teacher is Mrs jameson.
6. Our flute lessons start on thursday afternoon.
7. We went to covent garden to see the ballet swan lake
8. the creature my sister saw was a bat.

Punctuation One

Copy out these sentences, putting in the correct punctuation (full stops, capital letters, commas, question marks, speech marks, apostrophes, exclamation marks, colons and semi colons).

1. Louise went to rent a DVD she had £5 in her pocket
2. The film starts at 19 30
3. How many children have school dinners. Some children prefer to bring their own food.
4. Do you know which river runs through London
5. There were no pens in the drawer Ross had to go and look for one.
6. There was no sign of the spider in the house where could it have gone
7. Mum said, You'll be tired for school tomorrow if you play on your computer too late
8. Emily laid the knives forks and spoons on the table
9. We d never been to florida before
10. Oliver said call for me tomorrow at ten.

Spelling One

Which list has the correct spelling of the word?
Put a tick by the correct word.

A	B
monie	money
drew	drue
fingre	finger
field	feild
terrible	terrable
preety	pretty
warter	water
centre	center

Use of Language One

Write out the sentences, putting in the correct grammar. Which words are incorrect?

1. The boys throwed stones in the sea.
2. Mary feeled unwell at school.
3. This is the best sandwich I have ever eated.
4. The cat shook hisself when he came out of the water.
5. “My computer game is broke,” said the boy.
6. The trees is bare in winter.

Nouns can be singular or plural.

Fill in the blanks.

Most common nouns end in 's':		**Nouns ending in 's' 'ss' 'ch' 'x' 'sh' add es:**	
cow	cows	dress	dresses
shop	....	church	....
river	....	box	....
		bush	....
Nouns ending in 'y' add ies:		**Nouns ending in 'f' 'if' 'fe' add ves:**	
lady	ladies	elf	elves
city	....	life	lives
fly	....		
Nouns ending in 'o' add es:		**Learn the irregular nouns:**	
hero	heroes	ox	oxen
except musical terms...		deer	deer
piano	pianos		

Rewrite this passage.

1. First, change all singular words into plural.
2. Now, rewrite the passage in past tense.

A Country Scene

The child and his mother see a horse and a pony on the farm. At the end of the field, by the ditch, the sheep rests under the bush. The duck and the goose stay by the pond and the farmer's wife feeds the new born calf with a bottle. In the valley, a donkey brays loudly. He is startled by a lorry on the road.

Find the plural of these words.

Singular	Plural *(more than one)*	Singular	Plural
box	....	thief	....
brush	....	wolf	....
fox	....	chief	....
glass	....	hoof	....
watch	....	roof	....
army	....	cargo	....
city	....	echo	....
fly	....	hero	....
lady	....	potato	....
calf	....	day	....
half	....	piano	....
knife	....	valley	....
leaf	....		
loaf	....		
shelf	....		

Find the plural form of these words.

Singular	Plural	Singular	Plural
child	....	church	....
foot	....	cow	....
goose	....	life	....
man	....	pony	....
mouse	....	dress	....
ox	....	shop	....
tooth	....	donkey	....
woman	....	spy	....
brother	....	river	....
fish	....	hero	....
deer	....	elf	....
sheep	....	piano	....
trout	....	solo	....
box	....	shelf	....
bush	....	monkey	....

Exercise Two

Spelling

Which word has the correct spelling?

Put a tick in box A or B.

A	B
heard	hered
which	wich
afriad	afraid
frite	fright
dangurous	dangerous
grief	greif
atacked	attacked
tuch	touch
their	thier
bloon	balloon

Find five words to rhyme with the words below.

afriad or afraid	frite or fright	bloon or balloon
....	....	....
....	....	....
....	....	....
....	....	....
....	....	....

Practise your writing...

1. Remember the long summer holiday...

Choose one event or outing. Write at least twenty lines on your chosen subject. Make the account interesting by using as many details as you can.

2. September: Back to School

If you cannot describe an event or outing from your holiday, write down your thoughts about school, including as many details as possible. For example:

- new teachers
- friends
- work

> Always read through your writing.
>
> Ask yourself:
>
> - Have I written in sentences?
> - Have I remembered to use capital letters, full stops and other punctuation where needed?

Capital Letters Two

Write out the following sentences putting in the capital letters and full stops where needed.

1. Louise is taking grade one ballet but i am in the grade two class.
2. the hurt boy was taken to ashford hospital after the accident.
3. I go to my tutor, Miss Brown, on a thursday afternoon.
4. In Portsmouth, you can see the old ship the mary rose which has been raised from the bottom of the sea.
5. We went to see the dutch bulb fields last april.
6. The pantomime we are rehearsing is called cinderella.
7. We use fairy liquid to wash the dishes.
8. We had to pay a parking fine we parked on a double yellow line
9. The thameside hotel has a good restaurant
10. "have you done your homework, john?" asked the teacher.

Punctuation Two

Write out these sentences putting in the punctuation where needed.

1. The headmaster signed the letter A C Smith.
2. Many people perhaps hundreds waited to see the celebrity open the new leisure centre.
3. James wont forget to do his homework next week.
4. The boys mother shouted, Hurry up. You'll be late."
5. "Can you tell me the time" the lady asked the driver.
6. The film starts at 7 10 pm.
7. The leader told us to meet at 10 o clock.
8. It was damp dark and dusty inside the derelict house.
9. "Can I help you cross the road the man asked the old lady
10. Tom Wright the milkman is always cheerful

Vocabulary Two

Match the words with the correct meaning.

A and G - a .carriage is a vehicle with wheels.

A.	carriage	A.	alone
B.	surgery	B.	ability to do something well
C.	cancel	C.	skill of performing medical operations.
D.	ideal	D.	show how to do
E.	hurricane	E.	perfect
F.	reason	F.	wreck or ruin
G.	destroy	G.	vehicle with wheels
H.	solitary	H.	be content with
I.	exaggerate	I.	do away with
J.	satisfy	J.	the power to think and understand
K.	capital	K.	chief city
L.	skill	L.	gale
M.	explain	M.	to say something is better or worse than it is
N.	sympathy	N.	to have guests
O.	entertain	O.	person who plans, makes or looks after machines
P.	engineer	P.	share pain

Use of Language Two

Write out these sentences correcting the wrong words.

1. The apples is ripe on the tree.
2. "My toy car don't go," cried Sam.
3. The boy shouted to his friend, "You don't know nothing about football."
4. The rabbit run away when it was time to go back to its cage.
5. The proud boy congratulated hisself for winning the race.

Exercise Three

Vocabulary Three

Match the words with the correct meaning.

A.	depend	A.	fight
B.	struggle	B.	famous
C.	old	C.	necessary
D.	well known	D.	inside
E.	divide	E.	rely
F.	volcano	F.	a line of people
G.	essential	G.	mountain with a crater through which lava erupts.
H.	advertise	H.	fragrance
I.	interior	I.	antique
J.	procession	J.	having made up one's mind to do something
K.	stationary	K.	separate
L.	perfume	L.	let people know about
M.	determined	M.	standing still

Spelling Three

Which word has the correct spelling?

Put a tick in box A or B.

A	B
coming	comeing
leefe	leaf
ourselfs	ourselves
clock	clok
brief	breif
complane	complain
resirve	reserve
changeing	changing
appear	apear
parliament	parlament
rase	race
signed	sighned

Capital Letters Three

Correct these sentences.

Which sentences have capital letters where they are not needed?

1. The librarian explained, “madam, these books are overdue you will have to pay a fine.”
2. Joanne drove her car to old Windsor to see her granny.
3. The church produces a magazine called follow me.
4. The maori people come from New Zealand.
5. The moore family have sold their house they are emigrating to Australia,
6. how much is a bmx bike?
7. My dad has a volkswagon golf car.
8. The conference took place at bournemouth international centre.
9. At the convent school, sister mary taught history.
10. I asked my Father to help me with my homework.
11. I called, “dad, Help me! I am stuck.”
12. I asked my Sister Mary to play with me.

Punctuation Three

Correct these sentences.

1. It was raining on Thursday afternoon mum brought my umbrella to school.
2. I called to my sister, Are you ready”
3. I wont be able to come to the party.
4. “come over here I will sharpen your pencil for you, stated the teacher.
5. The film starts at 7 o clock.
6. The woman turned round and remarked, how are you I havent seen you for ages.
7. It is my brothers birthday on Wednesday.
8. The assistant opened her till and called please come over.
9. The girls mother worked at the airport.
10.

32 Sandringham Road
Rushford
July 4th

Dear Tom,

I am able to join you on Saturday at 2 30 pm. Look forward to seeing you.

Love,
Sam

Language Three

Correct the wrong words in these sentences.

1. There isn't nothing wrong with Marcus.
2. Sam didn't ought to go down the cliff.
3. Tom and I was waiting for the bell to ring.
4. The trainers I tried on feeled fine.
5. The strawberries is ripe. They are ready to be picked.
6. Lucy and me are good friends.

Revision

When nouns end in a vowel, ay and ey add s.

Make the following words plural:

monkey .... valley ....
holiday ....

These words are connectives: so, but, because.

Rewrite these sentences using connectives:

1. The fox chased the duck. He didn't catch it.
2. She had a bad cold. She stayed at home.
3. He could not go to the concert. He was unwell.

Remember: use who for animals and which for people.

Rewrite these sentences using who or which:

1. This is the winner. She scored the most points.
2. I stroked the cat. It belonged to my friend.
3. Tessa watched the bird. It sat on the fence.
4. The policeman stopped the young man. He drove the car without a licence.

Use Connectives

Rewrite the following sentences as one sentence, using the connectives below. You can use them more than once.

so	*when*	*where*	*but*
before	*while*	*who*	*so*
because	*yet*	*which*	*though*

1. He went into the house. He found a scared puppy.
2. Sophie was late for bed. She was watching TV.
3. It was raining. We went by car.
4. Paul was eating a sandwich. He saw a slug.
5. This is our new house. It was built last year.
6. Sophie could not drink her coke. She felt sick.
7. Laura searched for her book. She had left it at school.
8. Tom tried hard. He did not score a goal.
9. Dan began to feel hungry. He ate an apple.
10. Jasmit did his homework. He went to the cinema.
11. We saw the celebrity. He was opening the new store.
12. The sun was warm. It was Christmas Day.
13. Mum made a cake. Andrew washed the dishes.
14. Peter could not do the sum. He tried to understand.
15. She is very intelligent. She doesn't try hard.

Write out the sentences, completing them by choosing the correct homophone from the brackets.

1. My football cost £3.00 in the .... at the sports shop *(sail/ sale)*.
2. The bus .... to town is now £2.00 *(fair/fare)*.
3. The football team lost .... first match today *(their/there)*.
4. Please bring your book .... *(hear/here)*.
5. Emily wants to .... a poem *(write/right)*.
6. The teacher told the class to fetch the books and put them over .... *(there/their)*.
7. The trees are .... in the winter *(bear/bare)*.
8. The story is about a .... who fought on horseback *(knight/ night)*.
9. The old king had been a .... man *(grate/great)*.
10. My bicycle .... needs pumping up *(tyre/tire)*.
11. The boy, who wears glasses, has poor .... *(sight/site)*.
12. Tessa .... her old dress blue *(dyed/died)*.
13. On the way to the shops we pass .... the surgery *(by/buy)*.
14. I had finished my work .... I packed up *(sew/so)*.

Now, write sentences to show the meaning of the words you did not use.

Exercise Four

Capital Letters, Full Stops and Punctuation

Write out these sentences correctly.

Before you start,

a. find the sentence with no mistakes.

b. find the sentence which has a comma that is not required.

1. Last summer, we went to holland for a holiday we stayed at the hotel riviera the dutch people were very friendly.
2. Mum called, "Where has Olivia gone it is time for lunch."
3. Kelly called for me at 8 45 am but we did not arrive at school till gone 9 o clock. Theyd been held up in a traffic jam.
4. Class three will run a stall at the Rushford christmas Market on December 14th at 2 o'clock.
5. Joanne lives in Staines Middlesex.
6. Last February the heavy rains, left the field flooded.
7. On the bouncing castle we rolled bounced and fell over.

In these sentences, the comma and apostrophe have been over used. Write them out correctly.

1. Although the shop was closed, we could still see, through, the window.
2. My brother told me, to share the toys.
3. When, I pick up my rabbit, he scratches my hand.
4. That boy is the one, who won the competition.
5. Where, is my library book? It's title is The Lion, The Witch and The Wardrobe.
6. The flowers' look pretty in the garden.
7. The rehearsal for the play, will be on Thursday.

Remember, only use commas and apostrophes when you are sure they are correct.

The old house was damp, dark and dusty.

Lucy's book.

Spelling Four

Which word has the correct spelling?

Put a tick in box A or B.

A	B
cheese	chesses
stoped	stopped
fressing	freezing
any	eny
moter	motor
climing	climbing
hopeing	hoping
didn't	diden'nt
makeing	making
dropped	droped
tasting	tasteing
witch	which *not the one on the broomstick*
tossing	toseing
tipped	tiped
eventuelly	eventually
shopping	shoping
couldnt	couldn't
anywhere	enywhere
settel	settle
cirle	circle
pouring	poreing
payd	paid
packet	packit
persen	person

Vocabulary Four

Match the words with the correct meaning. Add two words of your own to this list. Write their meanings.

A.	excellent	A.	to look closely
B.	fiction	B.	to understand wrongly
C.	succeed	C.	make less
D.	record	D.	cold blooded animal
E.	mistaken	E.	person without courage
F.	coward	F.	....
G.	examine	G.	imaginary story
H.	heal	H.	keen
I.	eager	I.	hotness and coldness
J.	encourage	J.	essential
K.	release	K.	very good
L.	temperature	L.	petrified
M.	honest	M.	....
N.	reduce	N.	to do well
O.	reptile	O.	to praise
P.	terrified	P.	done at a fixed time
Q.	regular	Q.	information written and kept
R.	necessary	R.	to set free
S.	....	S.	fair
T.	....	T.	to make better

Language Four

Write the sentences out correctly.

1. We was given some homework on Tuesday.
2. We have bin to London to see the exhibition.
3. Emma she is nearly ten.
4. Us girls are all friends.
5. The teacher didn't tell nobody about the test.
6. Tom knowed he shouldn't pick the apples.
7. My tooths were aching.
8. My friend has went without me.

If these words were written in alphabetical order, which one would come first.

Decide which letter you need to look at in each group 1st, 2nd, 3rd or 4th before making your choice.

crocodile	....
butterfly	....
penguin	....
elephant	....

dinosaur	....
deck chair	....
dolphin	....
daisy	....

enemy	....
enjoy	....
enter	....
engine	....

orchestra	....
operation	....
observatory	....
oxygen	....

hotel	....
holiday	....
hovercraft	....
honey	....

exaggerate	....
examine	....
exact	....
example	....

Look up any words you are unsure of in a dictionary.

Synonyms are words with similar meanings.

Sophie finds English hard.

Which word below could be used instead of hard?

easy *wealthy* *difficult* *simple* *rich*

Can you think of some more?

Abbreviations are shortened words that have a full stop.

September - Sept.

Write the following words in full.

Feb. *Rd.* *AVE.* *Mr.* *Mrs.*

B.B.C *U.S.A* *U.K.* *O.H.M.S*

Contractions are shortened words.

it is - it's

Join the words together and write the short form.

he will *there is* *he is* *I am* *we are*

Can you think of some more?

Exercise Five

Spelling Five

Choose the correct spelling.

Put a tick in box A or B.

A	B
parcel	parsel
skurt	skirt
purse	perse
sadly	sadely
greif	grief
wilow	willow
agreed	aggreed
receive	recieve
leed	lead
resemble	ressemble

Capital Letters Five

Correct the following sentences, putting in the capital letters. Can you spot at least three capital letters that should not be there?

1. The post Office is in high Street.
2. The national eastminster bank stays open till four thirty now.
3. The Photographer from the informer newspaper came to rushford school last week.
4. He photographed the children who had participated in the knitting club. they knitted some squares to make a blanket for oxfam.
5. The advertisement claims that broclean washing powder washes whiter.
6. tom is the main character in the book tom's midnight garden by phillipa pearce.
7. Our new neighbours come from birmingham.
8. on Tuesday, gemma came to tea we had Fish Fingers and chips.
9. The bus stops in exeter road, by the Cinema, before turning right into fresco.

Punctuation Five

Correct the punctuation in these sentences.

1. Last August we visited friends in Reading Berkshire.
2. The teacher ordered, Stop talking."
3. It rained everyday during March April and May.
4. The piano recital will be given by Mary P Smith
5. Did you know that Miss Taylor is leaving at the end of the term
6. You shouldnt pick wild flowers in the countryside
7. Aunt Lorna was due to arrive at seven o clock but she didn't turn up till nearly 8 20 pm.
8. The little girl, put her hand out to stroke, the spotty dog.
9. The policeman found the girls green purse but her money had been stolen.
10. The boy shouted Where is my reading book

Use of language Five

Correct these sentences.

1. Mum promised she would learn me to cook.
2. The boy come to deliver the newspaper.
3. James knowed he was wrong.
4. Me and her go dancing on Tuesday.
5. The wind blewed hard last night.
6. Sue and I has to help the teacher.
7. We haven't never been to Paris.
8. Me and Louise are good friends.

Vocabulary Five

Match the words to the right meaning.

A.	memorise	A.	good looking
B.	mathematics	B.	happy
C.	guarantee	C.	study of science or number
D.	handsome	D.	something that is good to eat but rare.
E.	equip	E.	to cut to make a special shape.
F.	delicacy	F.	learn by heart
G.	delicate	G.	make longer
H.	cheerful	H.	promise to repair or replace
I.	interior	I.	without fail/ happen at fixed times
J.	expand	J.	easily harmed or broken
K.	regular	K.	to put together things that are necessary for doing something.
L.	soaked	L.	inside
M.	glimpse	M.	very wet
N.	canoe	N.	quick view
O.	carve	O.	long narrow boat
P.	pushed in a crowd	P.	jostled

Exercise Six

Capital Letters Six

Write the sentences with correct punctuation. Look for the sentences, which have capital letters where they are not needed.

1. The shop keeper asked, “can I help you madam.”
2. At the end of the Road, you will find Granny’s cottage.
3. I washed my hair with herbal essence shampoo.
4. The informer comes out on thursday.
5. Mum and dad are seeing my teacher on monday.
6. The japanese export many goods to great Britain.
7. I sent for a Catalogue from a mail order store.
8. we visited disney Land when we went to Florida.
9. The Flamingo is a bird that cannot fly.
10. Dick king-smith wrote a book called the sheep Pig.

Punctuation Six

Write the following sentences with correct punctuation. Look for sentences where punctuation has been used but is not needed.

To help you: use the semi-colon to separate two ideas not joined by a conjunction.

1. The lost property is in the secretarys office.
2. The cat was a stray. It’s fur was dirty.
3. The girls’ looked pretty in their party dresses.
4. Her grandma lived in Ipswich Suffolk.
5. My alarm clock rings at 7 am.
6. My cousin remarked “Are you coming for a walk.
7. The boy shouted at his mother, Where is my shirt”
8. Youll pass the test if you practise everyday.
9. Mr A C Jones is the manager at Berkleys bank.
10. We ran to the train station still we missed the train to town.

Vocabulary Six

Match each word to the correct meaning.

A.	calculate	A.	set free
B.	business	B.	facing
C.	suspicious	C.	a small person
D.	release	D.	to work out using numbers
E.	opposite	E.	keep biting
F.	dwarf	F.	to hang from above
G.	ointment	G.	trade and the getting of money
H.	scenery	H.	hotness or coldness of a place or object
I.	suspense	I.	feeling that something is wrong
J.	gnaw	J.	delay which frightens or excites people
K.	suspend	K.	substance used to heal a wound
L.	temperature	L.	painted background

Alphabetical Order Six

Which of these words would come first if they were placed in alphabetical order?

swan	....
model	....
bridge	....
tooth	....

toffee	....
umbrella	....
vegetable	....
title	....

guard	....
grow	....
good	....
gypsy	....

mixture	....
mischief	....
mind	....
mitten	....

polite	....
polish	....
police	....
pole	....

suspend	....
suspicious	....
suspect	....
suspense	....

Spelling Six

Place each word in the box below in the right sound family.

sentence	*boast*	*biscuit*	*stair*
handle	*witch*	*astronaut*	*relaxation*
cause	*teacher*	*boulder*	*naughty*

fence pence	throat coast	because pause	shoulder could ....
chair flair stair	fruit cruise	bought fought	station investigation ....
stitch pinch	reach beach	candle middle	daughter haughty ....

Use of Language Six

Correct these sentences.

1. Ben didn't ought to climb that tree.
2. They must speak more quieter.
3. He has ate his sweets.
4. Your friend has went on the bus alone.
5. These raspberries is sour.
6. Us girls played together.
7. The gasman come to mend the boiler.
8. Mark say to us to lend him a book.

Exercise Seven

Spelling Seven

Complete the sentences by choosing the right homophone.

boy *buoy*	*peace* *piece*	*red* *read*	*road* *rode*
made *maid*	*wait* *weight*	*bury* *berry*	*stake* *steak*

1. Melanie .... her book with the .... cover
2. The girl .... a horse along the ....
3. The dog will .... the bone under the bush with the red ....
4. The lady .... the .... clean the room.
5. I must .... for the doctor to check my ....
6. The .... saw the .... floating on the sea.
7. There was .... in the class, while the children made models from their .... of wood.
8. The gardener banged a .... in the ground before eating his .... and chips.

A child has written this passage. Rewrite the passage correcting the wrong spellings.

> My sister has bright red hare. She weres old tatty jeans that are to big. Ther are huge howls in the nees. She walks there dog every nite.

Now try this one.

> My ucle Jon has a long berd. He gose too work in his blak estate car. He has a gorgeous cat that he fed fish everyday.

Capital Letters Seven

Put in the correct punctuation and capital letters. Remember to take out the capitals that are not needed.

1. The man told me to turn right into fairbridge street.
2. This year the labour party conference was held in brighton.
3. By the river thames there is a beauty spot called Runneymede where king john signed the magna carta.
4. The bus stopped outside the Cinema before turning into the shopping centre.
5. I helped auntie jo by looking after my baby Cousin Jack.
6. The story of noahs ark is in the bible.
7. "Class eight went to visit the rushford gravel company on friday afternoon," said the headmaster.
8. on Sunday the girl guides attend Church Parade at st hildas baptist church.
9. The medal was awarded to sergeant davis he was wounded in Afghanistan.

Correct the following passage. Take out all the capital letters in the wrong place.

The night was very still there was a thin yellow Moon rising up over the Hill and the sky was filled with twinkling stars.

Late that night, after Chloe had gone to Bed. The soft kitten crept up on the duvet, curled up tightly and fell fast asleep.

Punctuation Seven

Put in the correct punctuation. Look for overuse of commas and apostrophes. Put in full stops, commas, exclamation marks and apostrophes where needed.

1. When the stray cat came towards us, We patted her gently. We didnt want to frighten her.
2. On thursday it was too wet to walk to school dad gave us a lift.
3. Sophies bookshelf was full of paperbacks she had read.
4. We cleaned we dusted and we polished the furniture. The room looked lovely when Mum came home.
5. The oven is heated we can cook the cake now.
6. "The homework is rather untidy this week" grumbled the teacher. that means you will have to do it again."
7. When Ellas photo was in the newspaper her mum bought the picture
8. The icing for the party cake, will be added on Thursday.
9. The boy shouted, "Help"
10. The boys' built a high tower with the bricks.
11.

Reading,
Berks,

Dear Kelly,

What time shall I come to tea on Thursday I am looking forward to seeing you again.

Your loving friend,

Jo

12. The football team has five good players: James Jack Adam Toby Josh.

Use of Language Seven

Correct the sentences:

1. Oliver brung me a present.
2. we saw squirrels in those trees.
3. I and Thomas work together.
4. "My glasses is broken," grumbled Liam.
5. Leave me to do my work.
6. I seed a ship on the horizon.
7. Give them little ones some sweets.
8. Our neighbour ask me to borrow him a bottle of milk.
9. The vet said the puppy hadn't nothing wrong with him.
10. Her elbow had wore a hole in the sleeve of her jumper.

Vocabulary Seven

Match each word to the correct meaning.

A.	pronounce	A.	announce
B.	precious	B.	line of people
C.	oxygen	C.	younger than
D.	original	D.	person who serves passengers
E.	approach	E.	valuable
F.	possess	F.	someone you do not know.
G.	junior	G.	allowing light to pass through
H.	procession	H.	to praise
I.	privilege	I.	not changing your mind
J.	steward	J.	to make the sound of a word
K.	stranger	K.	right or favour one can have
L.	transparent	L.	different from others
M.	worship	M.	have or own
N.	declare	N.	colourless gas
O.	stubborn	O.	come near

1. Find 5 words beginning with the letter P. Write them in alphabetical order.

2. Find 3 words beginning with S. Write them in alphabetical order.

Alphabetical Order Six

Write these lists in alphabetical order. These words are more difficult so take care.

whisker	....
whisper	....
white	....
whistle	....

salmon	....
sang	....
salt	....
sardine	....

torch	....
toffee	....
tortoise	....
toast	....

realise	ride	radio	round	rule
....	....	....	....	....

Correct the sentences by putting in the apostrophe:

1. The boys pencil lay on the floor.
2. The ladies coats were in the cloakroom.
3. My cousins hand was badly hurt.
4. The mens boots were covered in mud.
5. The childs shoe fell in the pond.
6. The register lay on the teachers desk.
7. He looked very smart in a firemans uniform.
8. It took several hours hard work to repair the damage.
9. The childrens books were left in my uncles house.
10. The maids dress was torn by a neighbours dog.
11. My fathers wallet was discovered in the thieves house.
12. A ducks egg is generally cheaper than a hens egg.
13. Mr Smiths watch is five minutes slower than Mr Browns.

Write these words as contractions using the apostrophe, as in ‘can’t’.

cannot	*could not*	*does not*	*do not*
he will	*I am*	*has not*	*did not*
have not	*he would*	*he is*	*I will*
is not	*I would*	*it is*	*I have*
of the clock	*over there*	*she is*	*shall not*
she will	*should not*	*that is*	*there is*
they will	*we will*	*we have*	*whatever*
wherever	*whosoever*	*who have*	*would not*
you will	*you are*		

Exercise Seven

Spelling Eight

What do you think is the correct spelling of these words?

smoth	*afriad*	*vewe*	*feild*
....	....	....	....
thier	*cirle*	*warter*	
....	....	....	

Correct the words that are spelt incorrectly.

1. The ship was moored to the boy.
2. I could here it loud and clear
3. Mum ordered me to practice my instrument, so I did three hours of flute practise.
4. My advise is to write to the council.
5. They rode into battel fearlessly.

Capital Letters Eight

Write these sentences out correctly:

1. Samantha's birthday is on christmas day.
2. the christmas lights in regent street have been switched on.
3. The queen prepared to meet the american dignitary at buckingham palace.
4. After Holly read the story of black beauty by anna sewell, she was determined to learn to ride.
5. The bbc programme blue peter is on Monday and Thursday.
6. The Teacher told my Mum that I was working hard at school.
7. The small village of cockington in south devon is a popular tourist attraction.
8. I had a favourite doll called lucy when I was three years old.
9.

Guildford, Surrey,

29th december.

Dear Auntie Joan,

thankyou for the lovely christmas presents you sent us. They will be very useful. We hope you had a happy Christmas.

Your loving nephew and niece,

Scott and Vicky

10. the president of the united states of america and the president of russia both attended the start of the arab, israeli peace conference which was held in madrid in november.

Punctuation Eight

Write these sentences out using correct punctuation:

1. The Librarian helped me to find the book I wanted.
2. Orlando the lost cat, that we read about in the newspaper has a new owner.
3. In grandmas jewellery box there is a very old necklace. Its very valuable.
4. The policeman grunted take care when you cross the road."
5. He advised Follow the road safety code Look left right and then left again If the road is clear walk slowly across.
6. The show went on tour during the summer months we saw it in London, last june.
7. It seemed to David driving his car over the flyover that the motorway was congested with heavy traffic.
8. Do you know what caused the accident

Correct the sentences:

After the new road opened a local resident stated my main concern is about the noise and general disruption the road will bring to us because of its close proximity to our homes.

Families in rushford are worried about the newly built road which will serve the new fresco store at rushford cross which is due to open on November 5th.

Now, write a letter to the local council expressing your concern about the new road that has been built near your home.

In the letter explain:

- where you live
- which road you are concerned about
- why it has been built
- when it will open
- why you are concerned about it.

Look up the meaning of these words in a dictionary.

attend	*conference*	*congestion*	*resident*
express	*concern*	*disruption*	*proximity*

1. Use them in a sentence.
2. List them in alphabetical order.

Write:

1. You are running a Christmas market. Write an advertisement giving details about it.

2. Now write a more detailed paragraph for the local paper or school magazine; giving details of when and where the event will be held, what will be for sale and any competitions or prizes.

3. Now imagine you are opening up a new restaurant or shop. Repeat the exercise above.

Vocabulary Eight

Match each word to the correct meaning.

A.	abbreviation	A.	to be able to pay for something
B.	admiration	B.	a person you have met but do not know well
C.	adjective	C.	a vehicle for carrying sick and injured people
D.	ambulance	D.	a fully grown person
E.	adventure	E.	a describing word
F.	advantage	F.	to think of with pleasure and respect.
G.	actual	G.	large and dangerous reptile
H.	acquaintance	H.	something that may help you get something you want
I.	adult	I.	real
J.	afford	J.	a shortened form of a word
K.	activity	K.	an exciting or dangerous journey or activity
L.	alligator	L.	something that is done

Alphabetical Order Eight

Write these words in alphabetical order:

fan	....
cactus	....
icicle	....
horn	....

daughter	....
dance	....
dangerous	....
date	....

beetle	....
bottle	....
bassoon	....
branch	....

explain	....
explode	....
expression	....
experience	....

passenger	....
passage	....
pasta	....
passport	....

themselves	....
theirs	....
therefore	....
they	....

transparent	transistor	transport	trainer
....	....	....	....

Use of Language Eight

Correct these sentences.

1. Jack can run more quicker than me.
2. Those kind of books are interesting to read.
3. Michael he is always late.
4. Tom and Amy has bad colds.
5. Sarah and she always play together.
6. You should learn your sister to swim.

ANSWERS

Page 8

I go to Castle Hill School.
My best friend is Paul.
There are three boys called Matthew in my class.
I live in Fairbridge Road in Kingston.
For my birthday treat I went to Lego Land in Windsor.
I like reading Harry Potter by J. K. Rowling.
In my road there is a church called Kingsbury Methodist Church.
Chloe and I went for a walk.
I go shopping on Friday with my mum.
In March it will be Easter.
Our new rabbit is called Benjy.

Page 10

When James went to London, he visited Buckingham Palace and The Houses of Parliament.

Page 16

Last weekend the two girls went to the theatre.
Emily raced across the road, without looking to see if there were any cars coming.
Due to the heavy rain, the fair was cancelled.
On the sea, the brightly coloured boats bobbed up and down.

Page 18

if, before, while, therefore, whereas, although, because, until

The show had an interval so that we could buy some refreshments.
The children were excited whenever it snowed.
I took my umbrella to the shops as it started to rain.
Sophie went on holiday to Spain although she did not like flying.
I could get some popcorn before the film starts.
We were arguing until Mum told us to stop.
I will help you with your homework if you tidy my room.
Rahan become very scared when he passed the creepy house.

Page 19

I visited the London Eye after I had been to the Tower of London.
I e-mailed my friend before I visited her.
Sam was happy as he was going on holiday.
Dad shouted at me because I broke the window.
I have refused to eat apples since I found a maggot in one.
My friend giggled when I dressed up as a clown.
I do not like fast rides so I do not go to theme parks.

Page 20

The crowd left the stadium after the match had finished.
I finished my homework on Friday, so that I could go out on the weekend.
I stood on a chair in order to see over the fence.
Work hard if you want to get good results.
I ate jelly and ice cream until I felt sick.
Sophie could not decide, so she bought both pairs of jeans.

Page 21

The boy won a medal, for rescuing his friend.
The girl apologised because she was late.
The cat purred softly when it saw its owner.
The class listened attentively while the headmaster spoke.
I stroked Becky's horse, as it leaned over the gate.
I can pick you up from the airport if you tell me what time you will arrive.
We observed the rescue helicopter hovering over the sea.
The old man was badly injured, so he was taken to hospital.
The robber was arrested for stealing jewellery.
The plane left on time, that was flying to Chicago.
Lucy shivered as she stood in the rain.
The celebrity looked glamorous wearing a red dress.
The mother put up a sunshade to protect the baby from the hot sun.
Sacha received an invitation to her friend's party.
The sailors sent up a flare as the ship was in trouble.

Page 23

"Would you like to come to my house for dinner?" said Darren.

Sophie slammed the door and shouted,
"It is not fair! Everyone else will be at the party." Her mum replied,
"You have not finished your homework."

Page 24

Is that your dog over there?
Your cat has caught a mouse.
Do you have any brothers or sisters?
What do you want to do when you leave school?
A policeman would be an exciting job.
Are you going abroad when you go on holiday?

Page 27

The girl's teddy was very soft.
Grandad's dog barked loudly.
Kim's jumper was itchy.
Sam's kite soared high in the sky.
Dad's car went very fast.

Page 28

the boy's pen
a day's work
the man's car
the woman's glove
the child's clothes

the ladies' bags
the boys' pencils
seven days' work

the women's gloves
the children's clothes

Page 29

can't – can not
couldn't – could not
don't – do not
didn't – did not
hasn't – has not
he'd – he would
haven't – have not
he'll – he will

he's – he is
I'll – I will
I'd – I would
I'm – I am
isn't – is not
it's – it is
I've – I have
o'clock – of the clock

shan't – shall not
she'll – she will
o'er – over there
that's – that is
shouldn't – should not
we'll – we will
there's - there is
they'll – they will
we've – we have

whate'er – whatever
where'er – wherever
whosoe'er – whosoever
who've – who have
wouldn't – would not
you'll – you will
you're – you are

needn't, you'll, I've, o'clock, don't, t'is

We'll probably arrive at seven o'clock.

Page 31

snored loudly
scribbled hurriedly
swooped aggressively
argued skilfully
waited expectantly
read eagerly
raced energetically
shouted angrily
crept cunningly
swayed violently

Adjective	**Noun**	**Verb**	**Adverb**
little, brown	mouse	crept	softly
huge, stripy	tiger	prowled	proudly
cute	rabbit	ran	playfully
ginger	cat	watched	attentively

Page 32

crept, gobbled, dozed, squeezed, croaked

stealthily, quickly, peacefully, awkwardly, loudly

Page 33

pretty garden
agreeable walk
interesting book
fine or pleasant morning
beautiful or pretty dress
fine house
fast car

delicious burger
naughty or mischievous toddler
enjoyable film

Page 36

The man shouted that he would help me.
The boy explained why he was late.
The girl whispered quietly to her friend.
The toddler screamed loudly.
The girl muttered that she was sorry.
I pleaded with Dad to let me go to the sleep over.

A road with many stones is a stony road.
A man of great wealth is a wealthy man.
A meal with a nice taste is a tasty meal.

Page 37

The wall was painted by the decorator.
The mouse was pounced on by the cat.
The car was driven by the racing driver.
The house was burgled by the robber.
The flood was caused by the heavy rain.

Page 38

(he), (her), (them), (yours), (mine)

Page 39

The cat pounced on the fence.
We chased my dog through the long grass.
Clare will be performing in the show.
The people crossed the road by the van.
He received a birthday card from his best friend.

Page 40

I'm ashamed of…
I took the blame for…
I will not comment on…
Compared to…
I was conscious of…
I disagree with…
I was disappointed in…
I am disgusted by…
He was guilty of…
I live opposite to…
He looks similar to…
She suffers from…
I will write to…
I will eagerly wait for…

Page 41

Since I went to my new school, I have learnt how to play the flute.
I attended the ballet classes until the end of term.
We know how the programme ended because we watched it.
We worked fast in order to finish the test.

He greeted me as if he had always known me.

Page 43

which, which, who, which

Page 46

as poor as a church mouse
as fit as a fiddle
as free as a bird
as right as rain
as wise as an owl
as thick as thieves
as safe as houses
as white as a ghost
as bright as a button
as black as coal
as big as an elephant
as alike as two peas in a pod
as cold as ice
as pleased as punch
as smooth as silk
as thin as a rake
as quiet as a mouse
as slippery as an eel
as dry as a bone

Page 50

see, sea
great, grate
blew, blue
right, write
knew, new
here, hear
break, brake
mail, male
peace, piece
flower, flour
meet, meat
son, sun
tale, tail
sew, so

Page 51

My new trousers are <u>blue</u>.
Beanos are my favourite <u>cereal</u>.
I cut a slice of <u>currant</u> cake.
I <u>hear</u> you are going on holiday.

Part Two

Page 53

cruel – brutal
stern – severe
not permanent – temporary
seldom – rarely

comfortable – cosy
just – fair
misery – suffering
expecting – waiting for
solitary – alone
explain – make clear
monstrous – enormous

Tim rides a brown horse. Its name is Lady.
The ship was warned of the dangerous rocks by the Portland Bill Lighthouse.
The book Wind In The Willows is written by Kenneth Graham.
Mum's birthday is on Valentine's Day, which is the 14th February.
Our new teacher is Mrs Jameson.
Our flute lessons start on Thursday afternoon.
We went to Covent Garden to see the ballet Swan Lake.
The creature my sister saw was a bat.

Page 54

Louise went to rent a D.V.D. She had £5 in her pocket.
The film starts at 19:30.
How many children have school dinners? Some children prefer to bring their own food.
Do you know which river runs through London?
There were no pens in the drawer. Ross had to go and look for one.
There was no sign of the spider in the house. Where could it have gone?
Mum said, "You'll be too tired for school tomorrow if you play on your computer too late."
Emily laid the knives, forks and spoons on the table.
We'd never been to Florida before.
Oliver said, "Call for me tomorrow at ten."

Page 55

money (B)
drew (A)
finger (B)
field (A)
terrible (A)
pretty (B)
water (B)
centre (A)

The boys threw stones in the sea.
Mary felt unwell at school.
This is the best sandwich I have ever eaten.
The cat shook himself when he came out of the water.
"My computer game is broken," said the boy.
The trees are bare in winter.

Page 56

shops, rivers
churches, boxes, bushes
cities, flies

Page 57

1) The children and their mothers see horses and ponies on the farms. At the end of the fields, by the ditches, sheep rest under the bushes. Ducks and geese stay by the ponds and the farmers' wives feed the new born calves with bottles. In the valleys, donkeys bray loudly. They are startled by lorries on the roads.

2) The child and his mother saw a horse and a pony at the farm. At the end of the field, by the ditch, the sheep rested under the bush. The duck and the goose stayed by the pond and the farmer's wife fed the new born calf with a bottle. In the valley, a donkey brayed loudly. He was startled by a lorry on the road.

boxes
brushes
foxes
glasses
watches
armies
cities
flies
ladies
calves

halves
knives
leaves
loaves
shelves
thieves
wolves
chiefs
hooves or hoofs
roofs

cargoes
echoes
heroes
potatoes
days
pianos
valleys

Page 58

children
feet
geese
men
mice
oxen
teeth
women
brothers
fishes
deer
sheep
trout
boxes
bushes

churches
cows
lives
ponies
dresses
shops
donkeys
spies
rivers
heroes
elves
pianos
solos
shelves
monkeys

Page 59

heard (A)
which (A)
afraid (B)
fright (B)
dangerous (B)

grief (A)
attacked (B)
touch (B)
their (A)
balloon (B)

afraid – (e.g.) made, laid, shade, paid

fright – (e.g.) might, night, sight, height, light

balloon – (e.g.) soon, maroon, tune, cartoon, afternoon.

Page 61

1) Louise is taking grade one ballet, but I am in the grade two class.
2) The hurt boy was taken to Ashford Hospital after the accident.
3) I go to my tutor, Miss Brown, on a Thursday afternoon.
4) In Portsmouth, you can see the old ship The Mary Rose, which has been raised from the bottom of the sea.

5) We went to see the Dutch bulb fields last April.
6) The pantomime we are rehearsing is called Cinderella.
7) We use Fairy Liquid to wash the dishes.
8) We had to pay a parking fine. We parked on a double yellow line.
9) The Thameside Hotel has a good restaurant.
10) "Have you done your homework, John?" asked the teacher.

1) The headmaster signed the letter A. C. Smith.
2) Many people, perhaps hundreds, waited to see the celebrity open the new leisure centre.
3) James won't forget to do his homework next week.
4) The boy's mother shouted, "Hurry up! You'll be late."
5) "Can you tell me the time?" the lady asked the driver.
6) The film starts at 7.10 p.m.
7) The leader told us to meet at 10 o'clock.
8) It was damp, dark and dusty inside the derelict house.
9) "Can I help you cross the road?" the man asked the old lady.
10) Tom Wright, the milkman, is always cheerful.

Page 62

(A) carriage – (G) vehicle with wheels
(B) surgery – (C) skill of performing medical operations
(C) cancel – (I) do away with
(D) ideal – (E) perfect
(E) hurricane – (L) gale
(F) reason – (J) the power to think and understand
(G) destroy – (F) wreck or ruin
(H) solitary – (A) alone
(I) exaggerate – (M) to say something is better or worse than it is
(J) satisfy – (H) to be content with
(K) capital – (K) chief city
(L) skill – (B) ability to do something well
(M) explain – (D) show how to do
(N) sympathy – (P) share pain
(O) entertain – (N) to have guests
(P) engineer – (O) person who plans, makes or looks after machines

Page 63

1) The apples are ripe on the tree.
2) "My toy car doesn't go," cried Sam.
3) The boy shouted to his friend, "You don't know anything about football."
4) The rabbit ran away when it was time to go back to its cage.
5) The proud boy congratulated himself for winning the race.

Page 64

(1) depend – (E) rely
(2) struggle – (A) fight
(3) old – (I) antique
(4) well known – (B) famous
(5) divide – (K) separate
(6) volcano – (G) mountain with a crater through which lava erupts
(7) essential – (C) necessary
(8) advertise – (L) let people know about
(9) interior – (D) inside
(10) procession – (F) a line of people
(11) stationary – (M) standing still
(12) perfume – (H) fragrance
(13) determined – (J) having made up one's mind to do something

Page 65

1) coming (A)
2) leaf (B)
3) ourselves (B)
4) clock (A)
5) brief (A)
6) complain (B)
7) reserve (B)
8) changing (B)
9) appear (A)
10) parliament (A)
11) race (B)
12) signed (A)

Page 66

1) The librarian explained, “Madam, these books are overdue. You will have to pay a fine.”
2) Joanne drove her car to Old Windsor to see her granny.
3) The church produces a magazine called ‘Follow Me’.
4) The Maori people come from New Zealand.
5) The Moore family have sold their house. They are emigrating to Australia.
6) How much is a B.M.X. bike?
7) My dad has a Volkswagon Golf car.
8) The conference took place at Bournemouth International Centre.
9) At the convent school, Sister Mary taught history.
10) I asked my father to help me with my homework.
11) I called, “Dad, help me! I am stuck.”
12) I asked my sister Mary to play with me.

1) It was raining on Thursday afternoon. Mum brought my umbrella to school.
2) I called to my sister, “Are you ready?”
3) I won’t be able to come to the party.
4) “Come over here. I will sharpen your pencil for you,” stated the teacher.
5) The film starts at 7 o’clock.
6) The woman turned round and remarked, “How are you? I haven’t seen you for ages.”
7) It is my brother’s birthday on Wednesday.
8) The assistant opened her till and called, “Please come over.”
9) The girl’s mother worked at the airport.
10)

32 Sandringham Road,
Rushford.
July 4th

Dear Tom,

I am able to join you on Saturday at 2.30 p.m. Looking forward to seeing you.

Love,
Sam

Page 67

1) There isn’t anything wrong with Marcus.
2) Sam (shouldn’t) (ought not to) have gone down the cliff.
3) Tom and I were waiting for the bell to ring.
4) The trainers I tried on felt fine.
5) The strawberries are ripe. They are ready to be picked.
6) Lucy and I are good friends.

monkeys, valleys, holidays

The fox chased the duck but he didn't catch it.
She had a bad cold so she stayed at home.
He could not go to the concert because he was unwell.

This is the winner who scored the most points.
I stroked the cat, which belonged to my friend.
Tessa watched the bird, which sat on the fence.
The policeman stopped the young man who drove the car without a licence.

Page 68

He went into the house where he found a scared puppy.
Sophie was late for bed because she was watching TV.
It was raining so we went by car.
Paul was eating a sandwich when he saw a slug.
This is our new house, which was built last year.
Sophie could not drink her coke because she felt sick.
Lara searched for her book but she had left it at school.
Tom tried hard though he did not score a goal.
Dan began to feel hungry so he ate an apple.
Jasmit did his homework before he went to the cinema.
We saw the celebrity who was opening the new store.
The sun was warm, yet it was Christmas Day.
Mum made a cake while Andrew washed the dishes.
Peter could not do the sum but he tried to understand.
She is very intelligent though she doesn't try hard.

Page 69

1) My football cost £3.00 in the sale at the sports shop.
2) The bus fare to town is now £2.00.
3) The football team lost their first match today.
4) Please bring your book here.
5) Emily wants to write a poem.
6) The teacher told the class, "Fetch your books and put them over there."
7) The trees are bare in winter.
8) The story is about a knight who fought on horseback.
9) The old king had been a great man.
10) My bicycle tyre needs pumping up.
11) The boy, who wears glasses, has poor sight.
12) Tessa dyed her old dress blue.
13) On the way to the shops, we pass by the surgery.
14) I had finished my work so I packed up.

Page 70

1) Last summer, we went to Holland for a holiday. We stayed at the Hotel Riviera. The Dutch people were very friendly.
2) Mum called, "Where has Olivia gone? It is time for lunch."
3) Kelly called for me at 8.45 a.m., but we did not arrive at school till gone 9 o'clock. They'd been held up in a traffic jam.
4) Class Three will run a stall at the Rushford Christmas Market on December 14th at 2 o'clock.
5) Joanne lives in Staines, Middlesex.
6) Last February, the heavy rain left the field flooded.
7) On the bouncing castle, we rolled, bounced and fell over.

1) Although the shop was closed. we could still see through the window.
2) My brother told me to share the toys.
3) When I pick up my rabbit, he scratches my hand.
4) That boy is the one who won the competition.

1) Where is my library book? Its title is 'The Lion, The Witch and The Wardrobe'.
2) The flowers look pretty in the garden.
3) The rehearsal for the play will be on Thursday.

Page 71

(1) cheese (A)
(2) stopped (B)
(3) freezing (B)
(4) any (A)
(5) motor (B)
(6) climbing (B)
(7) hoping (B)
(8) didn't (A)
(9) making (B)
(10) dropped (A)
(11) tasting (A)
(12) which (B)
(13) tossing (A)
(14) tipped (A)
(15) eventually (B)
(16) shopping (A)
(17) couldn't (B)
(18) anywhere (A)
(19) settle (B)
(20) circle (B)
(21) pouring (A)
(22) paid (B)
(23) packet (A)
(24) person (B)

Page 72

(A) excellent – (K) very good
(B) fiction – (G) imaginary story
(C) succeed – (N) to do well
(D) record – (Q) information written and kept
(E) mistaken – (B) to understand wrongly
(F) coward – (E) person without courage
(G) examine – (A) to look closely
(H) heal – (T) to make better
(I) eager – (H) keen
(J) encourage – (O) to praise
(K) release – (R) to set free
(L) temperature – (I) hotness and coldness
(M) honest – (S) fair
(N) reduce – (C) make less
(O) reptile – (D) cold blooded animal
(P) terrified – (L) petrified
(Q) regular – (P) done at a fixed time
(I) necessary – (J) essential

Page 73

1) We were given some homework on Tuesday.
2) We have been to London to see the exhibition.
3) Emma is nearly ten.
4) We are all friends.
5) The teacher didn't tell anybody about the test.
6) Tom knew he shouldn't pick the apples.
7) My teeth were aching.
8) My friend has gone without me.

butterfly, crocodile, elephant, penguin
daisy, deck chair, dinosaur, dolphin
enemy, engine, enjoy, enter
observatory, operation, orchestra, oxygen
holiday, honey, hotel, hovercraft
exact, exaggerate, examine, example

Page 74

Sophie finds English difficult.

February
Road
Avenue
Mister
Mistress
British Broadcasting Corporation
United States America
United Kingdom
On Her Majesty's Service

he'll
there's
he's
I'm
we're

Page 75

1) parcel (A)
2) skirt (B)
3) purse (A)
4) sadly (A)
5) grief (B)
6) willow (B)
7) agreed (A)
8) receive (A)
9) lead (B)
10) resemble (A)

Page 76

1) The post office is in High Street.
2) The National Eastminster Bank stays open till four thirty now.
3) The photographer from The Informer newspaper came to Rushford School last week.
4) He photographed the children who had participated in the knitting club. They knitted some squares to make a blanket for Oxfam.
5) The advertisement claims that Broclean washing powder washes whiter.
6) Tom is the main character in the book Tom's Midnight Garden by Philippa Pearce.
7) Our new neighbours come from Birmingham.
8) On Tuesday, Gemma came to tea. We had fish fingers and chips.
9) The bus stops in Exeter Road, by the cinema, before turning right into Frescos.

1) Last August, we visited friends in Reading, Berkshire.
2) The teacher ordered, "Stop talking!"
3) It rained everyday during March, April and May.
4) The piano recital will be given by Mary P. Smith.
5) Did you know that Miss Taylor is leaving at the end of term?
6) You shouldn't pick wild flowers in the countryside.
7) Aunt Lorna was due to arrive at seven o'clock but she didn't turn up till nearly 8.20 p.m.
8) The little girl, put her hand out to stroke the spotty dog.
9) The policeman found the girl's green purse, but her money had been stolen.
10)The boy shouted, "Where is my reading book?"

Page 77

Mum promised she would teach me to cook.
The boy came to deliver the newspaper.
James knew he was wrong.
We go dancing on Tuesday.

The wind blew hard last night.
Sue and I have to help the teacher.
We have never been to Paris.
Louise and I are good friends.

Page 78

(A) memorise – (F) learn by heart
(B) mathematics – (C) study of science/number
(C) guarantee – (H) promise to repair or replace
(D) handsome – (A) good looking
(E) equip – (K) to put together things that are necessary for doing something
(F) delicacy – (D) something that is good to eat but rare
(G) delicate – (J) easily harmed or broken
(H) cheerful – (B) happy
(I) interior – (L) inside
(J) expand – (G) make longer
(K) regular – (I) without fail/happen at fixed time
(L) soaked – (M) very wet
(M) glimpse – (N) quick view
(N) canoe – (O) long narrow boat
(O) carve – (E) to cut to make a special shape
(P) pushed about in a crowd – (P) jostled

Page 79

1) The shop keeper asked, “Can I help you madam?”
2) At the end of the road you will find granny’s cottage.
3) I washed my hair with Herbal Essence shampoo.
4) The Informer comes out on Thursday.
5) Mum and dad are seeing my teacher on Monday.
6) The Japanese export many goods to Great Britain.
7) I sent for a catalogue from a mail order store.
8) We visited Disney Land when we went to Florida.
9) The flamingo is a bird that cannot fly.
10) Dick King-Smith wrote a book called The Sheep Pig.

1) The lost property is in the secretary’s office.
2) The cat was a stray. Its fur was dirty.
3) The girls looked pretty in their party dresses.
4) Her grandma lived in Ipswich, Suffolk.
5) My alarm clock rings at 7.00 a.m.
6) My cousin remarked, “Are you coming for a walk?”
7) The boy shouted at his mother, “Where is my shirt?”
8) You’ll pass the test if you practise everyday.
9) Mr A. C. Jones is the manager at Berkleys Bank.
10) We ran to the train station; still we missed the train to town.

Page 80

(A) calculate – (D) to work out using numbers
(B) business – (G) trade and the getting of money
(C) suspicious – (I) feeling that something is wrong
(D) release – (A) set free
(E) opposite – (B) facing
(F) dwarf – (C) a small person
(G) ointment – (K) substance used to heal a wound
(H) scenery – (L) painted background
(I) suspense – (J) delay which frightens or excites people
(J) gnaw – (E) keep biting

(K) suspend – (F) to hang from above
(L) temperature – (H) hotness or coldness of a place or object

Page 81

bridge, model, swan, tooth
title, toffee, umbrella, vegetable
good, grow, guard, gypsy
mind, mischief, mitten, mixture
pole, police, polish, polite
suspect, suspend, suspense, suspicious,

fence, pence, sentence
throat, coast, boast
because, pause, cause
shoulder, could, boulder
chair, flair, stair
fruit, cruise, biscuit
bought, fought, astronaut
station, investigation, relaxation
stitch, pinch, witch
reach, beach, teacher
candle, middle, handle
daughter, haughty, naughty

Page 82

1) Ben (ought not to) (shouldn't) have climbed that tree.
2) They must speak quietly.
3) He has eaten his sweets.
4) Your friend went on the bus alone.
5) These raspberries are sour.
6) We played together.
7) The gas man came to mend the boiler.
8) Mark asked us to lend him a book.

Page 83

1) Melanie read her book with the red cover.
2) The girl rode a horse along the road.
3) The dog will bury the bone under the bush with the red berry.
4) The lady made the maid clean the room.
5) I must wait for the doctor to check my weight.
6) The boy saw the buoy floating on the sea.
7) There was peace in the class, while the children made their models from their piece of wood.
8) The gardener banged a stake in the ground before eating his steak and chips.

My sister has bright red hair. She wears old tatty jeans that are too big. There are huge holes in the knees. She walks their dog every night.

My uncle Jon has a long beard. He goes to work in his black estate car. He has a gorgeous cat that he feeds fish everyday.

Page 84

1) The man told me to turn right into Fairbridge Street.
2) This year, The Labour Party conference was held in Brighton.
3) By the River Thames there is a beauty spot called Runneymede, where King John signed The Magna Carta.
4) The bus stopped outside the cinema, before turning into the shopping centre.

5) I helped Auntie Jo by looking after my baby cousin Jack.
6) The story of Noah's Ark is in The Bible.
7) "Class Eight went to visit the Rushford Gravel Company on Friday afternoon," said the headmaster.
8) On Sunday, The Girl Guides attend church parade at St. Hilda's Baptist Church.
9) The medal was awarded to Sergeant Davis; he was wounded in Afghanistan.

The night was very still. There was a thin, yellow moon rising up over the hill and the sky was filled with twinkling stars.

Late that night, after Chloe had gone to bed, the soft kitten crept onto the duvet, curled up tightly and fell fast asleep.

Page 85

1) When the stray cat came towards us, we patted her gently. We didn't want to frighten her.
2) On Thursday, it was too wet to walk to school. Dad gave us a lift.
3) Sophie's bookshelf was full of paperbacks she had read.
4) We cleaned, dusted and polished the furniture. The room looked lovely when Mum came home.
5) The oven is heated; we can cook the cake now.
6) "The homework is rather untidy this week," grumbled the teacher. "That means you will have to do it again."
7) When Ella's photo was in the newspaper, her mum bought the picture.
8) The icing for the party cake will be added on Thursday.
9) The boy shouted, "Help!"
10) The boys built a high tower with the bricks.
11)

Reading,
Berkshire.

Dear Kelly,

What time shall I come to tea on Thursday? I am looking forward to seeing you again.

Your loving friend,

Jo

12) The football team has five good players: James, Jack, Adam, Toby and Josh

Page 86

1) Oliver brought me a present.
2) We saw squirrels in the trees.
3) Thomas and I work together.
4) "My glasses are broken," grumbled Liam.
5) Let me do my work.
6) I saw a ship on the horizon.
7) Give the little ones some sweets.
8) Our neighbour asked me to lend him a bottle of milk.
9) The vet said the puppy had nothing wrong with him.
10) Her elbow had worn a hole in the sleeve of her jumper.

Page 87

(A) pronounce – (J) to make the sound of a word
(B) precious – (E) valuable
(C) oxygen – (N) colourless gas
(D) original – (L) different from others
(E) approach – (O) come near
(F) possess – (M) have or own
(G) junior – (C) younger than
(H) procession – (B) line of people
(I) privilege – (K) right or favour one can have

(J) steward – (D) person who serves passengers
(K) stranger – (F) someone you do not know
(L) transparent – (G) allowing light to pass through
(M) worship – (H) to praise
(N) declare – (A) announce
(O) stubborn – (I) not changing your mind

Page 88

whisker, whisper, whistle, white
salmon, salt, sang, sardine
toast, toffee, torch, tortoise
radio, realise, ride, round, rule

1) The boy's pencil lay on the floor.
2) The ladies' coats were in the cloakroom.
3) My cousin's hand was badly hurt.
4) The men's boots were covered in mud.
5) The child's shoe fell in the pond.
6) The register lay on the teacher's desk.
7) He looked very smart in a fireman's uniform.
8) It took several hours' hard work to repair the damage.
9) The children's books were left in my uncle's house.
10) The maid's dress was torn by a neighbour's dog.
11) My father's wallet was discovered in the thieves' house.
12) A duck's egg is generally cheaper than a hen's egg.
13) Mr Smith's watch is five minutes slower than Mr Browns.

Page 89

cannot – can't
could not – couldn't
does not – doesn't
do not – don't
he will – he'll
I am – I'm
has not – hasn't
did not – didn't
have not – haven't
he would – he'd
he is – he's
I will – I'll
is not – isn't
I would – I'd
it is – it's
I have – I've
of the clock – o'clock
over there – o'er

she is – she's
shall not – shan't
she will – she'll
should not – shouldn't
that is – that's
there is – there's
they will – they'll
we will – we'll
we have – we've
whatever – whate'er
wherever – where'er
whosoever – whosoe'er
who have – who've
will not – won't
would not – wouldn't
you will – you'll
you are – you're

Page 90

smooth, afraid, view, field, their, circle, water

1) The ship was moored to the buoy.
2) I could hear it loud and clear.
3) Mum ordered me to practise my instrument, so I did three hours of flute practice.
4) My advice is to write to the council.
5) They rode into battle fearlessly.

Page 91

1) Samantha's birthday is on Christmas Day.
2) The Christmas lights in Regent Street have been switched on.
3) The Queen prepared to meet the American dignitary at Buckingham Palace.
4) After Holly read the story of Black Beauty by Anna Sewell, she was determined to learn to ride.
5) The B.B.C programme, Blue Peter, is on Monday and Thursday.
6) The teacher told my mum that I was working hard at school.
7) The small village of Cockington in south Devon is a popular tourist attraction.
8) I had a favourite doll called Lucy, when I was three years old.
9)

Guildford,
Surrey.
29th December

Dear Auntie Joan,

Thank you for the lovely Christmas presents you sent us. They will be very useful. We hope you had a happy Christmas.

Your loving nephew and niece,

Scott and Vicky.

10) The president of the United States of America and president of Russia, both attended the start of the Arab, Israeli peace conference, which was held in Madrid in November.

Page 92

1) The librarian helped me to find the book I wanted.
2) Orlando, the lost cat that we read about in the newspaper, has a new owner.
3) In Grandma's jewellery box, there is a very old necklace. It's very valuable.
4) The policeman grunted, "Take care when you cross the road."
5) He advised, "Follow the road safety code. Look left, right and then left again. If the road is clear, walk slowly across."
6) The show went on tour during the summer months. We saw it in London last June.
7) It looked to David, driving his car over the flyover, as if the motorway was congested with heavy traffic.
8) Do you know what caused the accident?

After the new road opened, a local resident stated, "My main concern is about the noise and general disruption the road will bring to us, because of its close proximity to our homes."

Families, in Rushford, are worried about the newly built road, which will serve the new Frescos store at Rushford Cross, which is due to open on November 5th.

Page 94

(A) abbreviation – (J) a shortened form of a word
(B) admiration – (F) to think of with pleasure and respect
(C) adjective – (E) a describing word
(D) ambulance – (C) a vehicle for carrying sick people
(E) adventure – (K) an exciting or dangerous journey or activity
(F) advantage – (H) something that may help you get something you want
(G) actual – (I) real
(H) acquaintance – (B) a person you have met but do not know well
(I) adult – (D) a fully grown person
(J) afford – (A) to be able to pay for something
(K) activity – (L) something that is done
(L) alligator – (G) large and dangerous reptile

Page 95

1) cactus, fan, horn, icicle
2) dance, dangerous, date, daughter

3) bassoon, beetle, bottle, branch
4) experience, explain, explode, expression
5) passage, passenger, passport, pasta
6) theirs, themselves, therefore, they
7) trainer, transistor, transparent, transport

1) Jack can run quicker than me.
2) Those books are interesting to read.
3) Michael is always late.
4) Tom and Amy have bad colds.
5) They always play together.
6) You should teach your sister to swim.

CPSIA information can be obtained
at www.ICGtesting.com
Printed in the USA
BVHW012225121118
532890BV00013B/588/P

9 780955 831553